P9-EMD-951

LANGUAGE AND LITERACY SERIES

Dorothy S. Strickland, Celia Genishi, and Donna Alvermann SERIES EDITORS

ADVISORY BOARD: RICHARD ALLINGTON, KATHRYN AU,
BERNICE CULLINAN, COLETTE DAIUTE, ANNE HAAS DYSON, CAROLE EDELSKY,
JANET EMIG, SHIRLEY BRICE HEATH, CONNIE JUEL, SUSAN LYTLE, TIMOTHY SHANAHAN

* Volumes with an asterisk following the title are a part of the NCRLL set: Approaches to Language and Literacy
Research, edited by JoBeth Allen and Donna Alvermann.

(Continued)

Children's Literature and Learning

LITERARY STUDY ACROSS THE CURRICULUM

Barbara A. Lehman

FOREWORD BY
Janet Hickman

Teachers College
Columbia University
New York and London

Published by Teachers College Press, 1234 Amsterdam Avenue, New York, NY 10027

Library of Congress Cataloging-in-Publication Data

Lehman, Barbara A.
    Children's literature and learning : literary study across the curriculum /
Barbara A. Lehman foreword by Janet Hickman.
        p. cm. — (Language and literacy series)
    Includes bibliographical references and index.
    ISBN 978-0-8077-4823-7 (pbk. : alk. paper) — ISBN 978-0-8077-4824-4
(cloth : alk. paper)
    1. Literature—Study and teaching (Elementary)   2. Reading (Elementary)
3. Children—Books and reading.   I. Title.
    LB1575.L36 2007
    372.64'044—dc22

                                                                          2007028942

ISBN 978-0-8077-4823-7 (paper)
ISBN 978-0-8077-4824-4 (cloth)

Printed on acid-free paper

Manufactured in the United States of America

14   13   12   11   10   09   08   07   8   7   6   5   4   3   2   1

To Dan,

who is both a true friend and a great reader

(with apologies to *Charlotte's Web*)

and my life partner;

to Hadley,

whom I have watched from birth grow into a reader;

and to Brett,

who is a sensitive reader of people

The Road Begins

(by J. Patrick Lewis)

It's the first day of 3rd
grade and we're sitting
in Mrs. B's classroom
that you would not believe
because the grains of sand
in the sea don't add up
to the books on her shelves,
a library gazillion of them
from Alice in Wonderland
to The Z Was Zapped.
And right there on Mrs. B's
door is a neon blue-green
sign in block letters—

READING BOOKS =

OK, ROAD BEGINS.

It's an anagram, she says.
She says, This is my house,
I live here and now you do, too.
There's magic in my house
that you'll remember for the rest
of your lives so choose a book
and open it to a page, any page,
until the index finger of your
imagination says, Whoa!
Then she pulls down a book,
starts reading it to herself,
and she's gone, far away,
I mean like Earth to Mrs. B.

Contents

Foreword

THE TERM *literary study* conjures up, for some, an image of dusty classics, single-answer questions, and total boredom. Happily, the literary study so ably detailed in this volume is something quite different, a vital and pleasurable pursuit of age-appropriate literature that allows readers to advance in a natural way from first impressions to richer understandings. Barbara Lehman describes a cyclical framework tailored for elementary classrooms that begins with reading and interacting with literature; moves on to the sharing of individual responses with other readers; and only then turns to promoting literary growth by giving explicit attention to terminology, narrative conventions, and knowledge *about* literature. Since beginning at this end point is such a common misstep and causes so many students to turn away from their inherent interest in stories, the author's insistence that experiencing and responding to literature come first may be her most crucial message.

It is easy to find books on teaching literature that offer descriptions of good practice, and it is not too difficult to locate discussions of theory. Volumes like this one, however, with its balance of serious attention to both, are something of a rarity. The opening chapters deal with literary and child development theories in the context of classroom literature teaching, making clear the connection between theory and a teacher's decisions. For additional help, the most relevant theories are explained in more detail in an appendix. In terms of practice, the author's recommendations draw credibility from multiple sources. She refers to an extensive base of research on literature in the classroom. She has taught many elementary teachers (both practicing and aspiring), learning from their experience, their questions, and their ideas. Yet the most compelling arguments for classroom practice usually come from those who have done it themselves. So it is significant that Barbara Lehman also brings to this work her own experience as an elementary teacher, one who has successfully used the methods and approaches suggested here and who can speak teacher to teacher about the results. She offers plain talk about the logistics of discussion groups, anticipates the questions and concerns other teachers might have, and issues sensible caveats as appropriate.

Perhaps the most provocative topic to come under the author's scrutiny is "skills instruction and children's literature" (the title of Chapter 4). The relationship between literacy learning and literary learning is more often talked around than talked about, so it is gratifying to find a discussion here that comes complete with lists and examples of the contributions of reading instruction to literary development and vice versa. Note especially Lehman's comments about conceptual pairs, which are processes or ideas from literary study and reading instruction that are essentially the same but carry different labels in their different camps, such as *intertextuality* and *prior knowledge* or *language* and *vocabulary*.

Children's Literature and Learning: Literary Study Across the Curriculum provides a vision for teaching literature and literacy as one, reconciling aesthetic and didactic approaches. Even better, it offers the beginnings of a road map for those who want to pursue all the richness of reading for their students.

—Janet Hickman

Preface

EARLY IN MY college education to become an elementary teacher, I took my first course in children's literature, and I was hooked. (This is not surprising, since I was an avid listener-reader [and reenacter] of literature from a very early age.) I realized then that what I most wanted to teach children was literature. I imagined a classroom in which young readers and I immersed ourselves in reading and discussing good children's books.

Unfortunately, as I progressed further in my teacher preparation program, I learned that vision was more fiction than reality. After that one literature class, there were no more like it, with the exception of a creative dramatics class in which we did dramatize literary texts. In particular, the reading methods class (which theoretically could have prepared me for *how* to teach the reading of literature) focused only on how to teach phonics, as far as I can recall.

My early teaching experiences reinforced this perspective. To my dismay, when I was handed the teacher's manual for the basal reader that I was expected to use with my students, I discovered that its emphasis was on comprehension and decoding skills and that the "stories" were not literature. With no guidance on how to make the link between teaching reading and reading literature, I struggled to work with my second graders, spending as little time teaching them *how* to read as possible (since I had received such useless preparation to teach reading and, unsurprisingly, viewed it as a chore to be avoided) and as much time as possible reading with and to them.

After 3 years, I decided to pursue my original love by entering a master's program that allowed me to concentrate for a glorious year on children's literature. Near the end of that program, one of my professors (who had greatly expanded my world of children's literature) looked me squarely in the eye and said, "Barbara, when are you going to study reading?" "Never, if I can help it!" I retorted.

I received my degree and went on happily to teach fourth graders for another 4 years in a setting in which I was able to teach lots of literature without too many unnecessary restrictions about following the adopted basal program. I learned (mostly intuitively) during those years that is *was* possible to teach reading through literature. However, eventually, my professor's words were replayed when I entered a doctoral program and, finally, decided to fill in the large gaps in my knowledge about reading instruction. That's when I discovered, while studying Louise Rosenblatt and Frank Smith at the same time, that literature and reading (ironically) were not incompatible!

For the past 21 years, I have been teaching undergraduate and graduate children's literature and literacy courses to present and future elementary and middle school teachers at Ohio State University. In these courses, I try to convey my belief that literary and literacy goals are both attainable. This book is written for teachers like I was early in my career. Beginning with the theoretical foundation from which such teaching practice is built, in it I demonstrate how to help children become skillful readers and writers who love literature.

This book would not have been possible without the support and guidance of certain individuals. First, I wish to thank two close, careful readers whose knowledgeable critiques from two different perspectives informed my thinking during the manuscript stage: Evelyn Freeman, professor of education and children's literature at Ohio State University, and Dan Lehman, professor of English at Ashland University. Second, I am indebted to Wendy Schwartz and other anonymous reviewers at Teachers College Press, whose valuable feedback made the final product much better yet. Finally, I want to acknowledge the unending support, patience, and tenacity of Carol Collins, my acquisitions editor at Teachers College Press. To these persons and you, my readers, I offer my heartfelt gratitude.

1

Theory and Framework for Literary Study with Children

TWENTY FOURTH-GRADERS huddle in four small groups to discuss a book they are reading together. Each group is reading a different book chosen from the set of book options I had given them. These are books such as *The Book of Three* (Alexander, 1964), *Tuck Everlasting* (Babbitt, 1975), *Bridge to Terabithia* (Paterson, 1977), and *Roll of Thunder, Hear My Cry* (Taylor, 1976). (See annotations in Children's Books Cited.) I had presented these choices during a book talk in which I introduced each book in one of various ways: relating it to another book they have read or to a familiar author or character, piquing their interest with questions—such as "Did you ever wonder what it would be like to . . . ?" and "Have you ever had an experience when you felt like . . . ?"—connecting the book to a recent event, reading aloud the first page or two, or asking a student who has read the book to give a one-minute "commercial." Often these book talks would focus on titles that were related in some way, for example, by genre or theme. (See Chapter 3 for a description of book talks.)

After the book talk, children had selected which book they wanted to read, with the only restriction being the number of children who could select each book. I rotate the order of children who are choosing, so that in each literature circle cycle different children get to pick first. Once they make their selections, they gather in their book groups for an initial meeting to explain why they picked the book, decide how much they would read for their next meeting, and start reading their books silently.

When they meet the next time in their literature circles, they bring their book and reading journals, first sharing something important they have written about the book in their journals, especially any questions they have about what they have read. The other group members respond to what is shared or asked, and often the literature discussion flows from there. Sometimes they get around to discussing the open-ended questions I provide for their book conversation, but this is not a requirement. I circulate among the literature groups, listening and even participating in the discussion. Mostly I try to share my own wonderings about the book, but sometimes I respond to something they bring up, using it as an opportunity to interject a literary concept that builds on what they are discussing if it seems to be a teachable moment. Other times, I make a note to myself to plan a lesson on the concept later.

Literature circles change when all groups have finished their books—about every 3 weeks or so—sometimes with culminating group presentations or some other product about their books. If a group finishes its book and project before other groups, there is plenty of individualized reading to occupy their time. In fact, every child is expected to be reading independently all the while. They have individual conferences with me about this reading and share their literary experiences in whole-class settings.

Granted, this teaching took place 25 years ago (and the books I mentioned have endured from that time period), but it was practice based upon theories that are still relevant today—along with more current ones referred to throughout this book—and important for us to use in our daily teaching. This book is about literary teaching that is developmentally appropriate for elementary students. In it I share specific ways that I and other teachers I know have implemented literary study in our classrooms, but the practices I describe are all based upon sound theories about literature and children's learning. They are in no way meant to be the "best" practices, but are examples that demonstrate how literary teaching can work in real classrooms.

THE CASE FOR THEORY

The foundation for good teaching is theory. Sometimes teachers have viewed theory as impractical and removed from the real practice of teaching, but nothing could be less true. As the language and literacy professor John Willinsky (1998) asserts, "Our practices exist by virtue of our theories" (p. 245), whether we like it or not. To ignore theories of literature is itself a kind of theory about the subject and does a disservice to our students and us. Instead, knowledge about various theories helps us to shape consciously our teaching practice. In today's political climate, theory is particularly important because it is much more flexible than a set of practices can be. A solid theoretical foundation enables us to be innovative and to create new practices adapted to changing realities without losing the grounding of sound principles.

For literary study, theory is important for us to help young readers engage with their reading and to make sense of it. When we experience a literary piece, our response is immediate and unique, but in order to make sense of these isolated experiences we have with literature, we need to step back and consider how that individual response fits within a larger picture. To do that, we use tools (theory) to help us think about our response and to identify relationships between individual works and their significance for our understanding of literature as a whole. "Theory is a way of getting up from among the words of a poem and asking what is it that allows language to hit one like that" (Willinsky, 1998, p. 250). Thus theory is the means to develop coherent structures out of discrete events; it helps us form a "story" about the stories we read.

However, literary theories are only one part of the story when it comes to children's literature—a term composed, significantly, of two words that are equally important. All literature must undergo the scrutiny of literary criticism and bear literary merit, and children's literature is no exception. But because the primary intended audience is children, it also must be claimed by children as theirs. This means that it must have child appeal. Adults can only judge the adequacy of child appeal by working with children, but adults also need to make sense of our interactions with children (just as we do of our interactions with books) by using theory to guide our understanding. In this case, our best sources are child development theories.

THEORIES UNDERLYING MY PRACTICE

To gain a more concrete picture of how good teaching depends upon theory, let's return to my class of fourth graders and examine what theories the practices I described exemplify.

- First, when children keep journals recording their ongoing responses to the books they are reading in small groups, this is an example of *reader response theory* (Rosenblatt, 1938/1995). Its emphasis on the reader's creating the literary work as a transaction complements Jean Piaget's theory of child development and learning that holds that children construct their own knowledge.
- Second, when I select the books from which my students will choose to read in small groups, I am mindful of their cognitive developmental levels and what I know about their psychological needs and interests. I try to provide a range of books that are appropriate for these

conditions, based upon *psychological theories*, which have close connections with Erik Erikson's psychosocial theory of child development as a process of encountering and working through important personality stages.

- Third, when these students share their responses with each other and hear each other's various perspectives, they are engaged in an interpretive community, in which the social context and children's cultural backgrounds influence meaning. These aspects of my practice exemplify *social and cultural theories*, which are informed by Lev Vygotsky's view of the social construction of knowledge in child development and learning.

- Fourth, *textual theories* help to guide my thinking and planning as I listen to book conversations and read individual journals. I notice the ways that my students' responses are influenced by the text, and I plan learning experiences that help them become aware of those influences. For example, if students who are reading *Bridge to Terabithia* mention the significance of the title and discuss with each other what they think it means, I can support their conversation by introducing the *concept* of the bridge as a literary symbol and the *term* to name this aspect of literature. (For explanation of literary terms used in this book, see the Glossary of Literary Terms in Appendix A.)

- Finally, *archetypal theory* (Frye, 1957) informs my thinking as I plan experiences that will encourage my students to make intertextual connections and begin to place individual pieces in the larger context of literature as a whole. For example, *The Book of Three* has many of the characteristics of a romance within the circle of stories (Sloan, 2003). Romance is a common form in children's literature, and understanding how this title fits the pattern can help readers see potential relationships with many other works.

For a fuller overview of the range of literary theories and explanation of the aspects of child development theories that best relate to the study of children's literature, see Appendix B.

A CYCLE OF LITERARY STUDY

In the context of theory, I envision a framework for the literary study I have described as a cycle of instruction. The framework is *not* a method, but rather a broad outline within which specific methods or approaches can reside. Thus the model is flexible and theoretical, while providing a structure for application. The three phases of the model link with the literary theories I have described, which together offer a valuable repertoire of tools for thinking about literary teaching and learning.

Phase 1: Reading and Interacting with Literature

This initial phase of the cycle, which can be associated with *reader response and psychological theories*, involves individual readers transacting with literature at particular points in their lives to create the "poem" or build the "envisionment" (Langer, 1995) that is, in at least some ways, unique to themselves. However, the transaction is not one-sided; the text also influences the reader in ways of which the reader may or may not be conscious. I will return to this consideration later when I describe how to promote literary growth in Phase 3.

Three key ingredients are needed for individual experiences with literature: wide reading, choice of what to read, and time to read and reflect. Award-winning author and critic Aiden Chambers (1983) states, "Wide, voracious, indiscriminate reading is the base soil from which discrimination and taste eventually grow" (p. 103); and according to Glenna Sloan (2003), noted expert on literary criticism with children, "Experiencing literature is the first step in the study of it" (p. 107). Books need to be available, and readers need to have access to them. Prescribed grade-level lists or even a "literary canon" should not dictate what books are available for children.

In a related point, children need to have choices about what they will read. While teachers and librarians must select (*not* to be confused with censoring) what books they will provide in their classrooms and libraries and use for literature circles, the range needs to be varied and extensive. Children need to be able to pursue their interests and discover new ones without being constrained by reading levels, a particular reading program, or the curriculum. Along with providing book choices, teachers need to give children many opportunities to browse through books and offer hints (but not rules) about how to choose books to read. Children also need the luxury of making inappropriate choices and abandoning books that they don't enjoy. These experiences can be very important in helping them to clarify what they do want to read.

Finally, children need ample time to select, read, and think about these books. Ardent readers are not created in tightly restricted schedules and 15-minute blocks of sustained silent reading. They need the time that it takes to learn how to choose books wisely. They need to be able to immerse themselves in books long enough to become absorbed and transported by the literary experience. They need time to reflect (through thinking or writing) about what they read on a personal, immediate level. Satisfying, engaging literary transactions don't happen on demand. As my fourth graders read their literature circle books or other self-selected independent reading, they are engaged in Phase 1.

Phase 2: Sharing Individual Responses to Literature with Other Readers

Moving from the more individual nature of Phase 1 to the more social quality of Phase 2 closely aligns the latter with *social and cultural theories* of literary study. Personal responses (in Phase 1) are the basis for a literary conversation that allows a community of readers to discover multiple perspectives, examine cultural influences, and build shared meanings. When my fourth graders convene their literature circles, they are participating in Phase 2.

As readers hear each other's unique transactions, they may encounter ideas that confirm, modify, or contradict their own insights. They discover that different readers respond to and interpret the same text differently, a realization that can broaden and deepen their own initial responses—or even cause them to wonder whether they have read the same piece of literature! For example, what do various readers make of the ambiguous ending of Lois Lowry's Newbery Medal winner *The Giver* (1993)? Do they think Jonas and Gabriel arrive safely at a destination where they can begin new lives and be loved? Or could these two characters' downhill sled ride at the end be a metaphor for their death? Or are there yet other interpretations? Sharing and listening to divergent responses often helps readers to become more conscious of their own ideas. Thoughts or feelings that may remain unrecognized while reading alone come to light when stimulated by someone else's insights. Finally, readers may wonder why others have such similar or different perspectives, which can lead to thinking about cultural effects.

Beginning with themselves, readers can examine what influences culture has on their responses. How do age, gender, race, ethnicity, religion, nationality, or class affect their readings and interactions with a particular literary work? For example, in light of my being a reader of Mennonite descent with some historical and religious understanding of the Amish, how is my response to *Gideon's People* by Carolyn Meyer (1996) influenced by my background experiences? This historical novel, set in Lancaster County, Pennsylvania, about an Orthodox Jewish boy who lives briefly with an Amish family, resonates with me because of my upbringing (Lehman, 2005).

After considering the implications of culture on our own responses, readers can try to answer the same questions about other readers. Even better, we can listen to others' ideas about these influences on themselves. Readers also should recognize who the author is and what his or her cultural background might be. What authority does the writer bring to the topic or themes? Again, to use *Gideon's People*, Carolyn Meyer was born in another area of Pennsylvania (Lewistown) with a large Amish population, and she is German American, as are the Amish. However, she claims no religious affinity to the Amish and researched the book through reading and visiting Lancaster County. These facts make me question her level of authority on Amish beliefs and practices and may explain what appears to me as a one-dimensional view of Amish life and beliefs.

Further, readers can try to detect which cultural or political assumptions that are held by the author may be inherent in the work itself and consider how these may interact with their own cultural or ideological assumptions. Equally significant, what gaps are in the text—what does the text omit—and what do those imply about culture or ideology? To continue with *Gideon's People*, what I perceive as the *absence* of positive family images, particularly in the Amish father-son relationship in contrast to the close one of the Jewish father and son, seems to be an unbalanced and rather unfair portrayal of these two devout groups.(Of course, one could argue that even the concept of "positive family images" is culturally constructed; that is, it privileges family over singleness. In addition, a "positive family" will be defined variously within different cultures.)

Noted children's literature scholars Perry Nodelman and Mavis Reimer (2003) call this "reading against a text" (p. 156), or resisting being manipulated to uncritically (or even unconsciously) accept the author's assumptions, especially if those assumptions are close to our own. This kind of reflection and discussion is important, because, as Jill May (1995), another literary scholar, notes, "If we wish to teach a generation of children how to appreciate cultural diversity, we must learn to go beyond consensus"(p. 180). Such critical analysis carries its own rewards and pleasures and gives readers power over what they read.

Sharing individual responses ultimately results in building joint meanings as a community of readers. While reading alone carries its own satisfactions, typically such reading is not as critical or in-depth as the shared interpretations that arise from discussion with others. Hearing other perspectives; evaluating, challenging, or accepting those; and defending or changing our own require more effort from readers. Reading becomes "pleasurable in different ways when a work's audience defines the beauties of a certain piece together and begins to suggest alternative ways of viewing a 'commonplace scene'" (May, 1995, p. 173). The camaraderie and sense of community that can develop from such conversations are exhilarating and reinforce the joys of reading. This kind of sharing also often requires tools (concepts) that facilitate literary discussions, leading to Phase 3 in the cycle.

Phase 3: Promoting Literary Growth

As readers interact with literature (Phase 1) and share their responses with other readers (Phase 2), opportunities and needs for literary growth arise naturally, such as I described with my fourth graders. Promoting such development often calls upon the knowledge and language of *textual and archetypal theories* and ultimately will enhance readers' literary transactions and interpretations. In this phase, I discuss how teachers can use teachable moments to educate children's responses, make interconnections between literary works, develop skills to become better readers and responders, and relate literature to other learning.

Teachable moments is a term used by educators to signify opportune, sometimes serendipitous, "just-right" times when a concept can be introduced and taught because some event or discussion or similar evidence shows that one or more children are ready to learn that idea. (Teachable moments are closely associated with Vygotsky's "zone of proximal development"—or the cognitive space within which a given child's learning most appropriately occurs.) Teachers can discover teachable moments by closely attending to children's responses to literature that are shared with other readers or conveyed in writing. By *closely attending*, I mean sensitively listening to what children say in discussions, how they say it, and what they *don't* say; reading response journals or other written responses; observing dramatic or artistic literary interpretations; and asking questions when aspects of response are unclear. (This topic will be addressed more fully in Chapter 7.)

Researcher Judith Langer (1995) suggests that a curriculum open to teachable moments is more "organic" than is a traditional, prescribed plan, but, according to her, is triggered by any of four situations that may occur in an instructional setting:

- Students have neither the concepts nor the language to talk about those concepts.
- Students have the concepts but not the language.
- Students have less complex understandings than their language implies.
- Students have the language and the concepts and are ready to think about these concepts in more sophisticated ways. (p. 123)

Teachers use their insights about children's literary development to ask questions, offer information, synthesize ideas, or plan future experiences that build upon present understandings to increase students' competence with and pleasure in literature.

For example, in research I co-conducted (Lehman & Scharer, 1995–1996), my coauthor and I found that young readers naturally made predictions about Sarah's intentions in Patricia MacLachlan's *Sarah, Plain and Tall* (1985), which signals an appropriate time to probe how they know Sarah will stay with the family she is visiting. One young reader supported this prediction by noting that Sarah left her cat and seashell collection behind with the family when she went to town by herself. Others observed Sarah's language: calling the haystack "our dune," including herself with the family by using words such as "we" or "us," and referring to their future together with such words as "later" and "soon." Teachers help children to form the *concept* of foreshadowing as they articulate ideas like these and, once that concept is established, introduce the terminology.

Literary criticism—the study of literature—is simply a form of educated response. While it begins with experiencing literature, it moves beyond that to conscious awareness of our responses to literature. Nodelman and Reimer (2003) offer ways in which teachers can promote this consciousness, such as encouraging children to ask questions about texts, make predictions, visualize characters and settings, evaluate texts, hear multiple perspectives of different readers, and record responses in journals. Rereading is another means; initial understandings and responses can be modified considerably in subsequent readings as students are able to notice different aspects of the literary work, especially after exposure to other readers' viewpoints, including the teacher's and even published critics'. We can read with new vision, and in this sense Rosenblatt's notion of the literary work being re-created anew each time it is experienced comes to fruition.

Teachers also can educate response by asking students to justify their interpretations. As Daniel Hade (1991), children's literature scholar, notes, "While accepting children's responses as honorable, literary teachers also push for rigor in their children's readings" (p. 11). This helps to sharpen their thinking and increase their "consciousness of response." Instead of simply acknowledging a reader when she states her dislike for a particular book, teachers will ask her why. For instance, to return to my earlier example about my response to *Gideon's People*, a teacher could challenge my thinking by inviting different readers' perspectives. (While my personal background may lend validity to my evaluation, it also may create bias in my reading, causing me to overlook other interpretations or to overreact to images that I perceive as troubling.) It also would be a good opportunity to consider whether authors are more obligated to present cultures (or religions) sympathetically or accurately and if they can accomplish both. In the process, as needed, teachers introduce literary terms and concepts that enable children to articulate their ideas more clearly and fluently. When children are ready, such knowledge empowers them as readers and responders and enriches their experiences with literature.

One concept that assists children to create their unique literary transactions is the recognition that texts have "gaps" that readers need to fill (Nodelman & Reimer, 2003). No story or poem tells the reader everything. Teachers are responsible for teaching children "gap-filling strategies" (p. 55) that help them to construct the "poem," or literary work. (However, gaps sometimes make assumptions about the reader's cultural and conventional knowledge—assumptions that may be erroneous and ideologically driven [Moon, 1999].) Such strategies include creating mental images of descriptions of settings and characters, getting to know the characters, following the story (chronology) and plot (ordered narration, but not necessarily chronological), discovering themes (the author's central ideas and purpose), identifying the narrator and point of view, and recognizing the text's structure (Nodelman & Reimer). Finally, readers can consider whether and how the work as a whole is consistent and believable. These are the traditional elements for literary analysis; they are central to textual theories. Learning about and using these strategies (at the appropriate time, namely, when they are ready) increases children's confidence about their reading and their understanding of new texts. Knowledge of literary concepts and language helps readers to think about why and how a piece of literature caused them to respond to it as they did. In other words, as I mentioned in my discussion of Phase 1, the literary transaction works both ways; readers can better understand the influence that the text also had on them.

As readers encounter more and more literature, they will be able to use their experiences with earlier readings to build envisionments (Langer, 1995) with increasing ease, because texts provide contexts for each other (Nodelman & Reimer, 2003). Readers may naturally recognize connections with texts they have read before, but children often need teachers' guidance and encouragement in making interconnections (known as *intertextuality*) between literary works. What a child may see as an isolated story can reveal itself in much richer ways when that piece of literature is compared with other works the child has read. As Sloan (2003) explains, "Literature is more than a collection of unrelated poems and stories" (p. 52), but in fact, has a coherent structure "as the continuous journal of the human imagination" (p. 47). Awareness of this wholeness of literature greatly increases the significance of literature.

I have already noted that teachers can help children to recognize the unity of literature by exploring archetypal patterns of romance, comedy, tragedy, irony, and satire that have roots in folklore, myth, and legend. For example, Patricia McKissack's *Flossie and the Fox* (1986) has echoes of "Little Red Riding Hood," with a clever twist in the way that Flossie outfoxes the fox. Other typical possibilities include the study of genres (for example, how are mystery stories alike or different?), variants of a folktale (Cinderella stories from many cultures, for instance), works by an author, plot or thematic structures (such as home-away-home, a common structural device), language patterns (such as repetition or conventional beginnings and endings), or topics (for example, friendship). The more that children interweave the literature that they read, the stronger and more intricate that literary tapestry will be.

When children gain consciousness of their responses to literature, use literary knowledge to articulate those responses with other readers, and build interconnections between literary works, they become better readers. However, like any endeavor that brings satisfaction, a solid foundation of underlying skills also is needed, so that children may become better readers (as discussed in Chapter 4). Skill proficiency alone does not create readers—only love for literature can do that—but it does make pleasure possible. Teachers are responsible for helping students develop skills that can help them to become better readers of and responders to literature.

Finally, literary growth can be promoted through exploring links to learning in other areas, such as social studies, science, or math (as described in Chapter 5). Just as there are interconnections between texts, so there also are literary relationships that readers can make with other subjects. Literary themes can be investigated through science (the cycle of life, the fragility of life and our environment, the impact of technology on nature, and so forth) or social studies (for example, characteristics of real-life heroes found in biographies, human beings' humanity or inhumanity toward each other, or how geography influences a sense of place). Mathematics can make literary interconnections with story or language patterns and sequences. These are examples of worthwhile ways to enrich literary experiences, but I will caution against the (over)use of literature to teach other subjects. Obviously, there are many ways that children's books can help young readers enjoyably learn about diverse topics, and while those practices can be very good, literature should be savored for its literary values first of all, not primarily as a means to teach information. With careful thought and skill, teachers can accomplish both appropriately.

Thus the cycle returns to its beginning, although it is not a simple progression. Each of the phases may lead to any other phase, so that the cycle may actually look more like an interwoven web in practice. In subsequent chapters, I will develop and describe the parts of this cycle of literary study more fully.

PURPOSE AND OVERVIEW OF THE BOOK

I believe that children are capable of true literary study if it is geared to their needs, interests, and experiences and honors their personal literary responses. I also believe that literary study and using literature for other curricular purposes are not incompatible. In other words, while we are teaching children *how* to read, we also can teach them how to read *literarily*; while we are teaching children subject matter, such as history or science, we also can instruct them how to appreciate the themes, language, and narratives of those topics. To *not* teach this way, I fear, risks marginalizing literature to the fringes of the curriculum or eliminating it entirely in a context of political mandates (and funding) to raise test scores. Literary values must be infused throughout our teaching practices.

The overall goal, then, is to demonstrate explicit relationships between literary theory and classroom application. My approach, I hope, will be practical, but with a solid theoretical foundation, and will fill gaps I see in what elementary teachers need and desire to become more knowledgeable and self-confident about creating literature programs for children. It also will support teacher educators who work with pre- and in-service classroom teachers to design such programs that accomplish curricular goals in literary ways.

In Chapter 2, I will explore the literary transaction in more depth (with extended examples from children's books to illustrate points), discuss the interaction between child development and literary learning, and examine the relationship between reader response and comprehension.

In Chapter 3, I detail instructional methods for literary teaching, such as reading literature aloud to children, giving book talks to children about literature, revisiting specific literary texts with children, leading literary discussions, encouraging children's response to literature through meaningful activities, designing and using teachers' guides appropriately, and creating small groups for both literature circles and teacher-led instruction.

In Chapter 4, I discuss the importance and place of literacy skills instruction in a literary classroom, how to promote both literary and literacy development simultaneously, and the appropriate place of basal readers and textbooks in a literary classroom.

In Chapter 5, I explore literature across the curriculum through literary qualities in nonfiction, the use of thematic units of instruction, multicultural and global education, and multilingualism.

I focus in Chapter 6 on creating a classroom environment for literary learning with the physical arrangement, a classroom library center, literature-related materials and equipment, schedules and the use of time, the social climate, and parent involvement.

In Chapter 7, I highlight the teacher's role in a literary classroom, including such factors as where the locus of control resides, decision making, and being a "curator" of literature.

Finally, in Chapter 8 I address how to get started and move forward in creating programs of literary study in elementary classrooms. I suggest developing and articulating a coherent philosophy; setting attainable goals; starting small and building gradually; dealing with inevitable concerns and frustrations; and above all, making these ideas work for you.

To that end, I invite you to join this exciting endeavor to explore how we can make our work with children rewarding both as the teaching and learning of literature *and* of the tools that make interactions with literature increasingly enjoyable, fluent, and meaningful.

2

Literary Learning and Children's Literature

THE INTEGRAL relationship between reader and text in a literary transaction (see Chapter 1) is captured in Ralph Waldo Emerson's comment, "Tis the good reader that makes the good book." Or as stated more colloquially by Nodelman and Reimer (2003), "A story or a poem doesn't exist until a reader makes it exist" (p. 52). While I noted that transactions with literature are central to Phase 1 in the cycle of literary study, Phases 2 and 3 are places to extend and deepen literary transactions, as well. Later in this chapter I will explore the relationships between children and literary learning, and between response and comprehension; but first, I focus on the literary transaction.

THE RELATIONSHIP BETWEEN READER AND TEXT

Louise Rosenblatt's theory (1938/1995) regarding literature as the lived-through *experience* between reader and text involves several considerations about that literary transaction, namely, aesthetic and efferent reading, literary criticism, and intertextuality.

Aesthetic and Efferent Reading

The first issue was addressed by Rosenblatt (1978) herself regarding the distinction between aesthetic and efferent reading. She describes aesthetic reading as an act in which "the reader's primary concern is with what happens *during* the actual reading event" (p. 24)—the thoughts, feelings, and sensations that one experiences in the moment. In contrast, efferent reading focuses the reader's attention primarily on what can be carried away from the event—what can be learned from or about the reading event (some of which, undoubtedly can enhance and illuminate past or future *aesthetic* reading events).

Thus, while the text (for example, its genre, topic, style, and so on) certainly influences every reading experience, the *reader's attention* determines whether the happening will be efferent or aesthetic. In addition, these two stances mark extremes of a continuum, along which a reader may vary his or her attention with the same text at different times or even during the same event. Rosenblatt argues that aesthetic evocation of literary texts should be primary and that analysis, which necessarily involves efferent reading, should follow later.

Literary Criticism

The next issue relates to literary analysis or criticism. When readers share responses to their readings (Phase 2), they need, first of all, to become conscious of their responses, which is the beginning of "stepping out and objectifying the experience" (Langer, 1995, p. 18). Responses evoked in an aesthetic reading may be subconscious initially, but readers must bring these to the surface so they can be shared. This awareness requires language (or other sign systems, such as art or music) in order for readers to articulate their perspectives, since that is the only way to convey lived-through experiences to a community of readers. Finally, they need to understand *why* they have the responses they do in order to explain or defend them when questioned by others. Knowing the reasons requires analysis and is the foundation of literary criticism.

I have already described literary criticism as a form of educated response. It employs a set of accepted conventions that facilitates analysis and ease of communication. As teachers, our job is to enable our students' literary experiences by teaching them the tools (conventions) they need to understand why a literary work causes them to respond as they do and the language they need to express their responses and reasons. This is Phase 3 of the cycle and should be central to reading instruction.

Furthermore, readers need to be exposed to others' responses, both as a way of broadening their own perspectives and for learning how to express responses competently. Written criticism is simply another reader's response and should be introduced at the appropriate time in readers' literary development. Students who have had their own responses received with respect and intellectual rigor will better understand that such criticism should be tested against their own experiences and evidence in the text and not accepted unquestioningly because it is published.

An Example of Literary Criticism

As an example, I share my analysis (adapted from Lehman and Crook, 1998) of *The Giver*, by Lois Lowry (1993), and Maurice Sendak's *We Are All in the Dumps with Jack and Guy* (1993). I employ literary elements and strategies to explore their meanings for me and use language to share my responses with you. Remember, however, that this is just one reader's interpretation and certainly not the only, or even necessarily a "best," one. (For example, see other interpretations of these books by critics and practitioners, such as Latham, 2002; Neumeyer, 1994; Sipe, 1996; and Sychterz, 2002.)

These two books—one a futuristic fantasy novel and the other a picture book of two nursery rhymes (see Children's Books Cited annotations)—might seem an unlikely combination, but pairing such books can stimulate especially unique insights and demonstrates that picture books are not just appropriate for young children. In fact, some, like Sendak's, invite relatively sophisticated analysis and interpretation. In addition, picture books require an interaction between text and illustration to create the literary work as a whole, and Sendak's book exemplifies well such interaction, as repeated references to the illustrations in this analysis will show.

Themes

Thematically, both books share a powerful sociopolitical vision of the condition of our world and the effect of its condition on our world's youngest citizens. Children are portrayed as society's victims, but both books also present children as the hope for the future. They may, as in Sendak's world, save themselves and create their own "family" or, as in *Giver*, use a child protagonist to save the community from a life devoid of decision making or human emotion. I see another theme about the nature of childhood revealed in these books. Sendak's view of childhood is anything but a time of innocent pleasures. Instead, many children face realities that range from homelessness, poverty, disease, abuse, and dysfunctional families to everyday insecurities and fears. *Giver*'s society has been "perfected" as an extended, idealized, but totally conformist juvenile state, ignorant of the darker realities of life. Still, through their child protagonists, these authors both demonstrate their respect for and faith in the resourcefulness of children and offer them hope for a better future.

The importance and meaning of memory is another theme that I find in both books. In *Giver*, the community denies memories of suffering and horror by entrusting them to one individual, the Receiver, so the rest of the community can remain blissfully ignorant. Likewise, Sendak shows us how society's castoffs are relegated to "the dumps"; thus, the unpleasantness of their existence is literally not remembered or noticed. Both authors allude to the dangers of such selective memory in creating conditions that can make otherwise unimaginable tragedies in history such as the Holocaust possible. Choice and responsibility for decisions is yet another theme these authors explore. *Giver* shows how following rules unquestioningly can be deadly and how, to truly live, they sometimes must be broken; while *We Are All in the Dumps* depicts how a group of unloved outcasts and orphans can unite to make choices that help them deal with common enemies and create their own rules in order to survive.

Language

Language is used in notable ways in both books. In *Giver*, language is used for control and is prescribed for every occasion. Terms are politically correct, uttered precisely the same way every time, and designed to avoid "unintentional lies"; yet ironically, they also are intentionally euphemistic, such as the use of "release" for "murder." Sendak, by contrast, uses language to be playful, suggestive, even shocking. Double entendres abound, with "dumps" meaning a trash heap or feeling dispirited; "trumped" (in a speech balloon) placed next to the word "Tower" on a building in the background that evokes the Trump Tower in New York City; and the juxtaposition of newspaper headlines about tragedies, such as AIDS and famine, with advertisements for "distinctive homes" and "smart living." Both books use language to reinforce and extend their themes.

Symbolism

Both books also are highly symbolic. For example, in *Giver*, the names of Jonas and Gabriel carry specific biblical connotations that may fit the book's themes of rescue or salvation, death, and resurrection (as exemplified especially in the story's ending). Jack and Guy's names may symbolize the opposite of particularity by being generic terms that can apply to anyone. Images of dumping and garbage are additional symbols found in both books. Sendak's society disposes of undesirables in the "dumps," where they will be out of sight and out of mind. Likewise, in *Giver*, elements and individuals who no longer have a place or use in the community are banished by their being sent "Elsewhere," and in the case of euthanized infants, literally dumped in the trash chute. Finally, in both books, nighttime and dream imagery play an important function, leading me to ponder whether *Giver* is a "nightmare" of a "dream" (utopian) world and *We Are All in the Dumps* is a "dream" of the "nightmare" world we may be creating. Both authors masterfully employ the dreamlike qualities of fantasy to convey their themes.

Structure

Structurally, both books constitute circular narratives. *Giver* is a quest that begins and ends in December, and the beginning foreshadows the ending. The dust jacket of *We Are All in the Dumps* suggests that the ending *is* the beginning, with placement of the title and author on the back of the book, and the last illustration echoes the first one by depicting the sleeping dump dwellers, bringing the story line full circle. In addition, the thematic, linguistic, and symbolic elements I've described all contribute to the books' structural integrity. The language and symbols reinforce the authors' themes to create unified literary works, and the illustrations in *We Are All in the Dumps* are crucial to the structure of that work as a whole. They provide the narrative's structure by giving the text layers of meaning, while the text provides the framework to develop two stories: Jack and Guy's adventure in saving the child and the sociopolitical subtext of society's treatment of its least fortunate members.

Pairing books such as these helps me to notice things about each that I might not recognize while reading them separately. John Beach (1993) also argues for the importance of comparing paired children's books "in order to make discoveries about the elements of literature and their impact on readers" (p. 383). He cites numerous examples of folktale or picture book dyads as further examples beyond my exploration of one pair.

Intertextuality

Analysis such as this allows a reader to organize responses in a way that helps one notice patterns, make literary interconnections, and develop intertextual insights—yet another consideration in the literary transaction. Not only are readers enriched by their interactions within a community of readers; experiences with texts are enriched by their place within the context of literature as a whole. Intertextuality, thus, becomes an ever more intricate web of relationships that readers develop between individual works they have experienced. Each individual text takes on greater significance when viewed as part of "an imaginative journal of all human experience" (Sloan, 2003, p. 70). Text-to-text connections help readers to not only understand and predict what might happen in a work they are reading currently—a positive contributor to child appeal (Lehman, 1986)—but also to gain new insights about texts read previously, according to researchers Shelby Wolf, Angela Carey, and Erikka Mieras (1996).

For example, children who have read one or more of Beverly Cleary's Ramona Quimby stories will more easily make predictions about what Ramona will do in another book because they have created certain expectations about her character and how she will act or think. Likewise, new understandings about Ramona may help readers resolve something that puzzled them about an action she took in a text read at an earlier time. Ultimately, readers develop schema, according to literary scholar Lawrence Sipe (2001), for Ramona Quimby stories, in particular, and perhaps for Beverly Cleary's style as an author, in general.

All this enhances readers' pleasure with their aesthetic transactions and "offer[s] children critical opportunities to build their own understandings" (Wolf, Carey, & Mieras, 1996, p. 151). Teachers can and should deliberately encourage these transactions by the way texts are juxtaposed with each other for reading and by the way interconnections are stimulated through conversations about and during read-alouds with books (Sipe, 2000). Thus, author or illustrator studies; explorations of genres, themes, or folktale variants; and other meaningful "text sets" play an important role in developing intertextuality.

"Literary Literacy"

All these considerations—reading with a specific aesthetic or efferent purpose, having the language and strategies to articulate responses, recognizing literary criticism as one kind of reader response, forming patterns and interconnections—are aspects of "literary literacy"—a term I borrow from scholars Mingshui Cai and Rick Traw (1997)—the achievement of which should be a major goal for instruction. "We should and can help students become competent readers of literature" (p. 24). Drawing upon the literary theories mentioned in Chapter 1 (and described in Appendix B), teachers can plan activities that help readers to develop increasing pleasure in their literary transactions, explains noted professor Richard Beach (1993). This requires teachers to know their students well by answering the following questions: What is their current knowledge about texts and literary conventions? What are the social and cultural contexts from which they come and within which they experience their reading? What are their past and present experiences to which they can relate their reading? Finally, what are the psychological and developmental factors that will influence their reading? Characteristics of children—who are represented by the first half of the term *children's literature*—are the focus of the following section.

CHILDREN AND LITERARY LEARNING

As noted in Chapter 1, child development theories (in concert with our own firsthand experiences with children) are the best sources of information about the characteristics of child readers. In Appendix B, I present the major theories and their relationships to the study of children's literature. Here I discuss more specifically the traits of developmental stages most relevant to teachers and how those attributes suggest certain features or types of literature that will be particularly meaningful and appropriate for children at different points of development. (For more detailed discussions and charts, see Huck, Kiefer, Hepler, & Hickman, 2004; Kasten, Kristo, & McClure, 2005.) Teachers should remember, however, that children need books that both meet them where they are at present and ones that push their horizons to new vistas.

Preoperational Stage

First, children in the preoperational stage (typically early childhood, approximately ages 2 to 4 years) are developing language ability rapidly. They have moved from speaking in single words to using phrases and simple sentences. Their speaking vocabulary shows particularly large increases around ages 3 and 4; their receptive vocabulary (what they understand) is even greater. Children at this stage also are egocentric; that is, they view the world and their experiences only from their own perspectives. They are the center of their universe. They learn best through firsthand experiences and play. They believe in magic, and "make-believe" is real. They tend to have short attention spans and to be highly active. While they are beginning to demonstrate more independence, they still need security and love from family. Their sense of time is limited, and their understanding of right and wrong is absolute.

Books that meet the interests and needs of children at this stage of development share certain characteristics. They tend to be short with simple plots and time sequences; to use repetitive language; to be illustrated with clear, attractive pictures; and to include characters and a point of view with which these young readers can identify. They are books that build upon children's firsthand experiences and that invite active participation such as movements or chanting along: simple alphabet and number books; stories about imaginary creatures and personified animals; books that portray young or small characters taking initiative while also being reassured that they are safe; and books in which good triumphs over evil. Specific examples might be *Goodnight, Moon* (Brown, 1947), *The Tale of Peter Rabbit* (Potter, 1902), *The Snowy Day* (Keats, 1962), *"More, More, More," Said the Baby* (Williams, 1990), *Lunch* (Fleming, 1992), *Knick-Knack Paddywhack!* (Zelinsky, 2002), and *Rosie's Walk* (Hutchins, 1968). (See annotations in Children's Books Cited list.)

Early Concrete Operational Stage

Children in the early concrete operational stage (approximately ages 5–7) are learning through hands-on, direct experience, and their language is developing more complexity and becoming more symbolic as they learn to read and write. Their interests and experiences are expanding, and they are becoming aware of perspectives different from their own and beginning to develop empathy for others. Their sense of fairness is very strong, and they want to see "wrong" deeds punished. Their sense of humor is developing, and their attention span increasing. Their desire for independence is growing, but they need to feel loved and secure with their parents and other important adults. Their response to stories is physical and imaginative.

Books that resonate well with these children may include fantasy; books that expand their firsthand experiences to new areas; books that provide reassurance that they can develop at their own pace; simple chapter books read aloud to them; and more complex alphabet and number books, such as *Alphabet Under Construction* (Fleming, 2002). Other titles for this stage might include *Leo the Late Bloomer* (Kraus, 1971), *Ira Sleeps Over* (Waber, 1972), *Flossie and the Fox* (McKissack, 1986), *Knuffle Bunny* (Willems, 2004), *Where the Wild Things Are* (Sendak, 1963), and *Not So Fast, Songololo* (Daly, 1985). (See Children's Books Cited for annotations.)

Later Concrete Operational Stage

Children from ages 8 to 11 are still typically in the concrete operational stage, but their thinking is more flexible, and they can assume more perspectives. Their language is becoming more complex as their experiences widen through more independent reading and writing. Reading abilities and interests grow increasingly varied, but humor is widely enjoyed. Peer-group acceptance gains importance, and children believe that they are as capable as adults and grow increasingly autonomous. Physical development varies widely, but children's coordination improves steadily. With some beginnings of puberty, gender identity strengthens. Understandings of morality become more subtle, and children gain a stronger sense of chronology.

Books for these children likely may include peer recommendations; longer chapter books and novels with strong plots and a fast pace; series books and books by favorite authors; adventure and survival stories; humorous books; biographies and historical fiction; informational books about specific personal interests such as sports or hobbies; books with multiple points of view and moral dilemmas; books with strong child protagonists who are competent at meeting challenges and solving problems; mysteries and more complex fantasy and science fiction; and books that show strong relationships with others and portray characters and settings beyond their immediate experiences.

Beverly Cleary's Ramona Quimby series portrays a favorite character who develops from a kindergartener into a fourth grader. The humor and predictability of these books hold considerable appeal for children in this stage. E. B. White's beloved *Charlotte's Web* (1952) incorporates animal-fantasy qualities that attract readers, but also portrays the development of Fern's character from that of a girl who still believes in talking animals to one whose interest turns more toward the opposite sex. Two books that stimulate thoughtful ethical and moral considerations among children who are beginning to grapple with such issues are *Tuck Everlasting* by Natalie Babbitt (1975) and *Shiloh* by Phyllis Reynolds Naylor (1991). Readers who seek fantasy and adventure may enjoy *The Tale of Despereaux* by Kate DiCamillo (2003), accompanied by an informational source about the time period such as *Castle Diary: The Journey of Tobias Burgess, Page* by Richard Platt (1999). For children at the upper end of this age range, *The Watsons Go to Birmingham—1963* by Christopher Paul Curtis (1995) portrays through humor and tragedy an important period of American history, the civil rights movement, and its effect on a Black family from Michigan. Finally, Jean Fritz's many biographies appeal to a wide range of interest levels, with her easy-to-read "question" biographies, such as *And Then What Happened, Paul Revere?* (1973), and the critically acclaimed Orbis Pictus award winner *The Great Little Madison* (1989). However, all her books are well researched and cite documentation information. (See Children's Books Cited annotations.)

Formal Operational State

The last stage of child development, formal operations, typically includes upper elementary and middle school ages of 12 and up. These children are rapidly turning into adolescents, but the age at which they reach puberty varies considerably. They are increasingly able to think logically and abstractly and to take multiple perspectives. The search for self-identity and purpose in life is strong, and they are becoming interested in issues of social justice and becoming aware of moral ambiguities. The importance of peers increases and creates pressure to conform. Sexuality becomes intensely interesting. Relationships and roles within families change but remain important issues and must accommodate these older children's need for independence while providing appropriate parental guidance. Language development becomes increasingly sophisticated in terms of vocabulary, syntax, usage, and symbolism. Children at this stage are more able to use language to think about literary concepts explicitly.

Books for readers at this stage may include high fantasy set in other worlds or futuristic fantasy; books with ambiguous endings; books that portray growing concerns and questions about sexuality and sexual preferences; books about the search for personal identity; books that show young people coping without adults; and books that deal with social and moral issues and peer relationships. Lloyd Alexander's Prydain Chronicles, set in the fantasy medieval kingdom of Prydain, not only provide exciting plots and themes about the nature of good and evil, but also feature a protagonist, Taran, who matures from an impetuous boy whose only interest is in pursuing adventure into an adolescent who seeks his personal identity, and finally a young man who finds romance and accepts his responsibility as a leader. Gary Paulsen's *Hatchet* (1987), a straightforward adventure story of a 13-year-old boy, provides ample opportunities for readers to imagine the possibilities of living without companionship or adult assistance. *Holes* by Louis Sachar (1998), *The Giver* by Lois Lowry (1993), and *The Friends* by Kazumi Yumoto (1992) offer rich examples of moral and social dilemmas that may intrigue readers at this stage. *The Giver* also will challenge students to consider the ambiguities of its conclusion. In Lesley Beake's *Song of Be* (1993), the naïve young Be gradually loses her childhood innocence as she matures into a young adolescent, who like Julie/Miyax in *Julie of the Wolves* (George, 1972) realizes her parent is not the perfect person she once thought. Jacqueline Woodson's *From the Notebooks of Melanin Sun* (1995) portrays how a 13-year-old boy deals with his mother's same-sex relationship and his dawning awareness of his own sexuality. For an exploration of the horror and heartache of war, even one as idealized as the American Revolutionary War, readers can debate issues raised in *My Brother Sam Is Dead*, by James Lincoln Collier and Christopher Collier (1974). Uri Orlev's award-winning *The Island on Bird Street* (1984) depicts a boy's survival of war in the Jewish ghetto of Warsaw, Poland, during the

Holocaust and invites empathy for children whose lives are severely altered by the effects of hatred and injustice. Finally, Naledi, in Beverley Naidoo's *Chain of Fire* (1990), exemplifies how a 13-year-old girl can join the struggle against an evil apartheid system to protest the forced removal of Blacks from their homes. (See annotations in Children's Books Cited.)

A Word About Gender Preferences

As stated above, children's gender identity strengthens with age and development; thus it is logical to assume that a relationship will develop between gender and reading interests. Children's literature experts Barbara Kiefer, Susan Hepler, and Janet Hickman (2007) examine research on gender factors that influence children's reading preferences and find the evidence mixed. Some studies have shown that boys tend to develop a preference for nonfiction over fiction at an early age, and that both genders classify books as "boy's" or "girl's." Furthermore, girls will read a "boy's" book more often than boys will read a "girl's" book. Other research, however, shows the diversity of children's reading preferences across both genders and substantial similarity between boys and girls on topics, authors, and genres. What seems important for teachers to do is to include a wide variety of books that appeal to all children and to include children in the process when classroom reading materials are selected. In particular, boys—who, as they grow older, are found in some research to show less interest in reading overall—should be encouraged to participate in book selection.

A Few Cautions

Developmental theories about childhood have much to offer educators about children and their literary learning. However, I conclude this section with several cautions:

1. "Guides for ages and stages," as they are sometimes called, are just that—guides, not prescriptions. Individual children can and do develop at their own pace and with their own preferences.
2. The titles I've identified as examples are merely suggestions of the *kinds* of books that may appeal to children. Do not limit your (or children's) selections to just these; read widely, become acquainted with the broad range of works available, and compare them with the characteristics of literature that children at a given level of development likely might find appealing.

3. Finally, always remember that children come from diverse social and cultural contexts that strongly influence their needs and interests. They benefit from not only books that reflect their lives and experiences, but also ones that provide windows through which to view the life experiences of others, according to Rudine Sims Bishop (1994), noted scholar of children's literature. Both kinds will provide them with self-affirmation and with empathy for those whose lives are different.

With an understanding of the literary transaction and variables regarding children's development and their literary learning, we turn now to the relationship between response and comprehension. This is a critical link for teachers whose first preoccupation may be with *literacy* rather than *literary* learning and development.

RESPONSE AND COMPREHENSION

Research by Joyce Many and Donna Wiseman (1992) suggests that when it comes to aesthetic or efferent readings of literature, students often respond first to the lived-through experience (Rosenblatt, 1978) of reading a narrative text. Other research has examined the types of child readers' responses and has found commonalities. Lehman and Scharer (1995–1996) defined two broad categories (with additional subcategories in each): reader-based responses "related to the personal feelings, personal values and preferences, and connections made by the reader to experiences or other reading" (p. 145) and text-based responses focused on analysis and interpretation "in relation to the literary elements and literary structure of the text and the author's crafting of it" (p. 145). We further learned that child readers tended to respond first in reader-based ways and then later made text-based responses. Sipe's (1997) research used essentially these same two broad categories and further categorized children's literary responses in storybook read-alouds (1998) as the following: analytical, intertextual, personalizing, transparent, and performative. Of these, the last four would correspond to reader-based responses, while the first would be text based as defined by Lehman and Scharer.

Still other research has shown that children's response types change with development, as summarized in Huck, Kiefer, Hepler, and Hickman's well-known textbook on children's literature (2004). Janet Hickman's (1981) research showed that young school-age children (kindergarten and Grade 1) responded to literature with body movements and by acting out favorite stories or types of characters. Children in Grades 2 and 3 responded by reading and sharing insights together. Older elementary children (Grades 4 and 5) engaged intensively with their reading, sometimes forgetting their surroundings while being engrossed in a story. Huck and colleagues (2004) further explain that younger children respond to parts of stories, often by retellings and by using language that assumes the listener knows the story context. Middle elementary readers do more summarizing of stories and begin to classify them into some of the same categories used by adult readers, such as mysteries and fantasy. They evaluate books based upon their personal reactions and may borrow elements from their reading to use in their writing. Older elementary and middle school students exhibit pronounced preferences in their reading and can generalize ideas from a story to a broader context. They are more analytical about stories and can begin to understand a connection between the way works are written and their feelings or reactions to them.

This connection between readers and texts is the *literary* transaction, but it also has been viewed by *literacy* researchers and theorists as the heart of reading. Frank Smith (1996) and others describe reading as an interaction between a reader and text, specifically, the reader asking questions while engaging with a text and comprehending (constructing meaning) when those questions are answered. Readers' literary responses provide "evidence" of their comprehension (Rosenblatt, 1991, p. 447); indeed, their responses are the only means by which teachers, through observation and interaction, may learn about students' comprehension, which should be a central concern in fostering and evaluating their development of literacy. Thus, I argue, a dichotomy between literary and literacy learning is false and counterproductive. Such polarities lead to unnecessary schisms in literacy education and to teachers being caught between teaching literacy skills or nurturing literary enjoyment and understanding.

What I will demonstrate in the following chapters is how teachers can do both—nurture pleasure and teach skills—*simultaneously* and eliminate most anxieties about attending to one while neglecting the other. In Chapters 3 through 5, I will explore how, to reverse Emerson's aphorism, teachers can use good books throughout the curriculum to make good readers, children who develop a lifelong love for reading and consciousness about themselves as readers.

3

Instructional Methods for Literary Teaching

THE DIFFERENCE between literary and nonliterary *literacy* instruction has much to do with both *what* teaching methods are selected and *how* they are used. In the previous chapters, I have laid the foundation in theory and research for what I hope will create the understanding teachers need regarding literature and children. In this chapter, I will explore practical ways to bring the two together so to develop lifelong readers. The practices that I believe are essential in this endeavor include reading aloud to children, giving book talks, revisiting texts, leading discussions by asking thought-provoking questions, encouraging response by offering meaningful activities, using teachers' guides appropriately, creating groups, and conducting literature circles and instructional groups.

READING ALOUD

One important way to invite children to enter Phase 1 of the cycle of literary study is to read aloud to them. Teachers can share their pleasure in literature through the texts they choose and how they read those pieces. If teachers select books that they love and that they believe can appeal to children and if they read them with joy and enthusiasm, children will catch that spirit. Teachers also serve as good models of reading, not only demonstrating the pleasure they receive from reading but also reading with fluency and expression to make literature come alive for their listeners. The works teachers select to read aloud can expose young readers to excellent literature—particularly books that children may not be able or ready to read for themselves—that helps to refine their literary taste and broadens their horizons. Children discover new authors and illustrators, genres, and topics that pique their interest. They hear new words and familiar language used in fresh, intriguing ways that increase their verbal abilities and are aesthetically pleasing. Exposure to well-written stories builds children's sense of story and their understanding of how different text structures work, both of which contribute to strong comprehension. The shared experience of hearing the same piece of literature helps to foster a sense of community in a classroom as the listeners discuss what they are hearing and how it relates to their own lives, according to former teacher educator Virginia Allen (1995). Extensive research at least as far back as Dorothy Cohen's (1968) solidly supports that reading aloud to children "significantly improves their vocabulary knowledge and their reading comprehension" and "can affect reading interests and . . . language development" (McCormick, 1977, p. 139). In fact, reading aloud has been identified as "the single most important activity for building the knowledge required for eventual success in reading," according to the often cited report *Becoming a Nation of Readers* (Anderson, Hiebert, Scott, & Wilkinson, 1985, p. 23).

Planning and carrying out successful read-alouds are not difficult; and they may be spontaneous, but they are not haphazard. First, teachers select with care what to read. With my fourth graders, I chose books that I enjoyed, above all, and that I thought these children would appreciate. I tried to find books that connected with their interests and experiences and that enhanced or widened those in new directions. I always read these books first to myself so that I would be thoroughly familiar with the content. If my selection was a picture book, I practiced reading it while holding the book so that the child audience could see the illustrations while I read. Most children are naturally curious and will be dissatisfied if pictures are turned away from their view while they are listening. Furthermore, my experience showed that children (even in the upper elementary grades) will listen best and become most engaged when I had them gather around me on a comfortable carpeted area away from their desks and other distractions. This physical grouping was a signal to give their attention to what I was reading to them. It also was more intimate and relaxed.

There are numerous suggestions from researchers and educators about the best techniques for reading aloud to children. Often, especially for works read at a single sitting, an introduction sets the stage by linking the piece to a current topic of study or other relevant, timely experiences; for example, one book to consider would be *Snowballs*, by Lois Ehlert (1995), which would be read on the occasion of the first snowstorm of the season. For longer novels or books read over a series of read-aloud sessions, inviting one student to briefly recap what was read the previous time helps the audience to focus their thoughts and prepare to listen. Asking children to make predictions about the story or selection to be read can be good motivation for attentive listening.

During the read-aloud, depending on my purposes, I may invite children's participation by pausing at various points to allow for questions, comments, or predictions, or I may decide to read straight through to the end of the selection or segment before inviting such responses. In any case, we need to save time at the end for listeners to first make their own comments before starting any directed questioning. (More on this topic later.) We also need to be sensitive to and aware of the students' backgrounds. Choosing literature that connects with specific cultural contexts and encouraging children to bring their cultural knowledge to the conversation enhances everyone's experience. For example, Jeane Copenhaver (2001) learned in her research with African American children during read-alouds that creating a safe environment in small-group settings where they could respond physically during the session led to richer literary connections. By contrast stifling interruptions or unprompted dramatizations muted these children's engagement. Sipe (2002) also describes the importance of "expressive engagement," which includes five types of response during read-alouds that teachers may view as too disruptive or subversive but that demonstrate true pleasure and passion with literature. Teachers need to be open to ways of interacting that are different from those traditionally favored in many classroom environments.

Children require structure and routine, but variety also is good for learning, so while it is important for teachers to read aloud every day to their classes, these listening-to-literature events can both be scheduled regularly (after lunch or recess, for example) and be spontaneous occurrences. In addition, we should vary what we read aloud to our students; children enjoy and need to hear poetry and informational books in addition to narrative literature. Poetry is best read aloud to appreciate the rhythms and sounds of its language, and exposure to a wide variety of genres is the most natural way to learn and experience them. Often I would link these selections thematically to the fiction I was reading aloud to the class. The wonder and beauty of the first snowfall can be enhanced by reading not only *Snowballs*, but also poetry that celebrates the event, such as Alice Schertle's *All You Need for a Snowman* (2002) and learning some of the science of snow in a biography such as Caldecott Award winner *Snowflake Bentley* (Martin, 1998). (See annotations in Children's Books Cited.) Finally, in the years that I taught kindergarten through fifth grade, I never found that my students were too young or too old to enjoy and benefit from my reading aloud to them. Indeed, these are some of my most treasured memories with those classes, and I hope they are avid readers today.

BOOK TALKS

By reading aloud, I couldn't possibly share all the literature with my students that I wanted and needed to. Giving book talks was another way to bring good literature to their attention. Book talks are like short sales pitches and should provide just enough information about the books to entice children to read them. Usually I would select some titles related to one that I had read aloud. These might be books that were by the same author or illustrator, that were of the same genre (such as biographies or mysteries), or that were thematically or topically related (books about journeys, for instance).

Once I had gathered these books, I would organize my remarks about them in some logical fashion, emphasizing intertextual connections between the books and with the book I was reading to the children. I would develop some kind of teaser to entice the children, perhaps posing a question about their own lives and then introducing the books. Or I might read aloud selected paragraphs or scenes to pique their interest, stopping at an exciting point that might draw them into the text. (See Figure 3.1 for a sample book talk.) I always made these books available for the children to read, and in my experience, they were immediately claimed. Those readers, in turn, made excellent story "sellers" to other readers, and so the love of books spread.

REVISITING TEXTS

Anyone who has read to children can relate to the situation in David McPhail's (1987) *Fix-It!* in which young Emma begs her parents to read a book to her again and again—even after the television is "fixed." Actually, this is sound pedagogical practice for promoting children's literary development. Revisiting books by reading them multiple times allows readers to notice things that aren't recognized the first time through, when most readers, and especially children, attend to a book's plot. It is during these revisits that students will (and we can encourage them to) think about how the plot is structured or how the characters develop or the way that language contributes to style or how the author used foreshadowing to make us anticipate certain events. Rereading helps readers to move past initial responses and to reconsider texts, particularly in light of insights and perspectives shared by other readers.

Rereading also contributes to children's literacy growth. Once read, texts are more familiar, and thus easier to read. Children need a blend of both new material that challenges them and old favorites that allow them to practice their developing literacy skills and solidify their understandings. Researcher

Mary Jo Fresch (1995) learned that "rereading generally indicated a confidence-building time" (p. 125) for first graders, but it also holds merit for older readers. Repeated readings of familiar books and stories allow for building fluency, according to reading educators Jean Wallace Gillet, Charles Temple, and Alan Crawford (2004)—in short, for practice to make perfect. Fluency and confidence makes reading much more pleasurable and satisfying.

Literary criticism offers good opportunities for teachers to learn "literary strategies for reading children's literature" (May, 1995, p. 9) and to gain teaching ideas for inviting children back into previously read texts (Nodelman & Reimer, 2003). For example, Jinx Stapleton Watson (2001) discusses how Jack Gantos's character Jack Henry demonstrates the archetypal hero in a series of books (*Heads or Tails*, 1994; *Jack's New Power*, 1995; *Jack's Black Book*, 1997; *Jack on the Tracks*, 1999) that follow the classic quest cycle: home-adventure-home. This same pattern is found in numerous other literary works with heroes ranging from Odysseus to Peter Rabbit, Watson argues, and helping children to recognize such universal elements leads to understandings about story structure and invites them to find connections with other stories they read. A teaching strategy for developing this insight is to read other books with the same structure or to review other stories with which the students are already familiar and then diagram the plot structure in a circle shape divided by the number of main events (determined by the children) of the story. If this is done across several stories, students easily will see the similarities and understand the common structure, an insight that will enhance their sense of story.

Likewise, British researcher Pat Pinsent's (2002) idea that Louis Sachar's *Holes* (1998) is a modern fairy tale that can be used with older children who are already very familiar with the fairy tale genre to help them appreciate how fairy tales deal with human nature, the sometimes harsh realities of life, and the struggle between good and evil and still result in a happy ending. Students can generate a list of the characteristics of fairy tales, then an analogous list of the characteristics of *Holes*, and compare the two. They can use the comparison to draw conclusions about the nature and purpose of fairy tales and the role of modern stories in this tradition. Revisiting texts in this manner is the heart of Phase 3 in the literary cycle.

LEADING DISCUSSIONS

During and after read-aloud sessions and as another means to revisit these works, I tried to promote my students' literary engagement, insights, and

Figure 3.1. Sample Book Talk About Families and Belonging

I am reading Pam Muñoz Ryan's award-winning *Becoming Naomi León* (2004) to a fifth-grade class. This book deals with the need of children—Naomi and her younger brother Owen—(who are not living with their biological parents) to know who their parents are, while also feeling loyalty and love for their great-grandmother, who has raised and cared for them. It is about discovering one's identity and place of belonging. The story is set in California and Mexico and revolves around the Mexican festival of La Noche de los Rábanos (the Night of the Radishes). I want to invite my students to explore these and related themes in similar novels, so I introduce them to the following books in this manner.

❧

Pictures of Hollis Woods, by Patricia Reilly Giff (2002). This Newbery Honor book is about a 12-year-old girl, Hollis Woods, who was abandoned as a baby and has lived in a variety of foster homes her whole life. She is now staying with Josie, an old woman, after running away from a family who loved and wanted to adopt her. Josie, who was a former art teacher, also loves Hollis and recognizes Hollis's artistic talent, but she is becoming increasingly forgetful and unable to care for Hollis as she should. Why did Hollis run away from the Regans, who made her feel so happy and loved? What is she going to do about Social Services when they find out about Josie's condition? Where will she be sent then? In a series of flashbacks, prompted by memories associated with pictures she has drawn, we learn about Hollis's life with the Regan family and the events that caused her to leave them. These alternate with chapters set in the present about her life with Josie and show how, in the end, the two stories come together.

Saffy's Angel, by Hilary McKay (2002). Saffy (short for Saffron), the second of four children, who are named after paint colors, in an artistic, unusual family, accidentally discovers that she is adopted. This is very upsetting to Saffy and makes her feel that she doesn't really belong where she is. Her real mother, the twin of her adopted mother, lived in Siena, Italy. What happened to her mother? Why didn't anyone tell Saffy she was adopted? Why did her grandfather give her an angel statue when he died? What is the connection of the angel to her own past? How can she travel to Italy to seek the answers to these questions, and what happens when she does? This book from Britain shows that young people in another country share many of the same concerns and worries as those of children, like Naomi León, in the United States.

Locomotion, by Jacqueline Woodson (2003). In this Coretta Scott King honor book, Lonnie Collins Motion (aptly nicknamed Locomotion) is an 11-year-old living with a foster mother, Miss Edna. His teacher, Ms. Marcus, persuades him to write down his mixed-up thoughts and feelings about his life. Why is Lonnie living in a foster home away from his younger sister, Lili? What happened to their parents? How can he be rejoined with Lili? What kind of foster parent is Miss Edna? Lonnie's life gradually unfolds in a series of free-verse poems in which he discovers his ability as a writer and what a family can be. Lonnie shares many similar issues with Hollis Woods.

Buttermilk Hill, by Ruth White (2004). Another young poet discovers her talent in this novel, set in a small North Carolina town in the 1970s. Piper Woods is 10 years old when her parents decide to divorce, leaving her to wonder where she belongs as they move on with their lives. Meanwhile, she and her best friend, Lindy (who also is her father's youngest sister but just Piper's age), make a new friend, Bucky, who has his own troubles, including a mystery about his parents, as Saffy does. How does Piper feel when her dad remarries and adopts his new wife's twin sons? How does she feel about her mother going back to college? Why is Bucky's mother so crazy, and what is she writing that she keeps from Bucky? Who is Bucky's father? Over a period of 4 years, Piper learns to deal with all these situations and work out her feelings of loss, anger, and confusion through writing poems that eventually earn her an important reward.

These five books, all appropriate for approximately the same age range of readers, will engage students in exploring questions about what makes a family, about where the characters belong, and about dealing with life's realities. Readers can select which book they want to read, discuss their responses to the book in their book group, and then compare and contrast their book with the books read by other groups. In this manner, one reader's insights will be enriched by others', perceptions about one book will be viewed in new light through comparisons with other books, and readers will get recommendations from their peers about books that interest their friends.

understandings through leading discussions—or stimulating conversations, which might be a less didactic way to describe them. I prepared for these experiences by paying attention to my own thoughts as I read the material. What are my questions? What causes me to wonder? These responses are the best bases for genuine (as distinct from "teacher-like") questions—those for which I did not have the "right" answers, although I probably had some thoughts. For example, in discussing *The Well* (Taylor, 1995), I might ask about the differences between the characters Hammer and David. Why and in what ways are they so different? What purposes do these different characters serve in the story? I might ask about plot expectations. Did you expect the plot to develop the way it did? Why or why not? What caused you to react that way? Finally, from a sociocultural point of view, I might wonder how this story might be different if it had been written by a White author, for example, in terms of language or perspective.

I concentrate on questions that invite deeper thinking about the story and that require inference, interpretation, analysis, application, or evaluation. I phrase questions so they cannot be answered with yes, no, or one right answer, and I avoid either-or questions, because they not only stifle higher-level thinking but also inhibit good discussions. I also remember that children who can competently discuss higher-level questions are exhibiting good comprehension. They don't need to answer lower-level questions for me to know that. In wording questions, I have found that it helps children to realize that I don't have specific, "right" answers in mind (that they need to guess) if I insert the words "do you think" into the question. For example, with Ian Falconer's *Olivia* (2000), I might ask children about the author-illustrator's use of color (something that I have pondered) in the pictures. Phrasing the question as "Why *do you think* the illustrator used only the color red (and pink) other than black and white in the pictures?" signals that I really do want to know what the students think, not just for them to guess what I think. Then I also have to give them enough time to think, which may require some waiting.

Sloan (2003) has detailed how teachers can develop questions to help children explore and grasp the forms and structures of a story (see pp. 142–149) and to generalize literary principles, such as conventional characters and imagery (see pp. 155–170). Children's-literature authority Patricia Cianciolo (1995) proposes a progression of questions to build on children's "initial affective and cognitive response to literature" (p. 147); to focus on specific aspects of the piece of literature; and finally, to "direct attention to the context in which the selection(s) is (are) encountered—a context of other readers, other texts, and personal history" (p. 148). Former classroom and reading teacher Joy Moss (2002) provides an in-depth treatment of the art of questioning and types of questions and when to ask them, such as prior to, during, and following reading a text. These concepts are all aspects of literary literacy and will help young readers gain the tools they need to increase their understanding of and pleasure in literature. They also "help students explore possibilities, not merely to resolve uncertainties" (Langer, 1995, p. 58).

Finally, we need to remember two guiding principles: (1) start with the children's responses and build the discussion from there, and (2) encourage "grand conversations," a term coined by Ralph Peterson and Maryann Eeds (1990), in which the students talk to each other, not in answer to our questions.

First, alert teachers can accomplish many objectives simply by paying attention to what children notice and by shooting "literary arrows" (Eeds & Peterson, 1994, p. 23) at the appropriate moment that connect to what children say and linking that to literary concepts with specific terminology. Listening to what children notice gives us good insights about their readiness to learn certain ideas and the developmental appropriateness of those concepts. For example, in answer to my question about whether readers expected *The Well*'s plot to unfold as it did, they might point out such incidents as David stating that he listened to his father's advice while Hammer didn't or Charlie Simms suggesting that if Hammer got too "prideful" about his family's well, someday the Logans might "find somethin' dead floatin' in it" (p. 25). Once students have noted these, then I can introduce them to the term *foreshadowing* to give them a name for this literary device. This is one of those teachable moments in which students have shown that they "have the concepts but not the language" (Langer, 1995, p. 123) and I can facilitate their literary development.

Second, when students talk to each other, not primarily in answer to our questions, the conversation may become a genuine inquiry. To encourage this, teachers need to do more listening; give children more time to think and to respond to each other; share our own wonderings, not our certainties; and support with further investigation their search for answers to remaining or new questions.

ENCOURAGING RESPONSE THROUGH MEANINGFUL ACTIVITIES

Children's interactions with literature also can be greatly enhanced by offering young readers varied and meaningful activities that encourage their responses. I propose experiences that lead them *back into* the story, rather than away from it, and invite them to engage with it in a creative manner that can develop imagination and deeper insight. To pass my test of "leading back into the story," the activities will be ones that can be done only if the children have heard or read the story. For example, with Peggy Rathman's *Officer Buckle and Gloria* (1995), having children develop a list of safety tips for their own classroom does not require having read the text, nor does it particularly develop deeper insights about the story itself. However, having readers write a letter to Officer Buckle or Gloria (as children did in the story) about their favorite safety tip in the story and suggesting another tip that Officer Buckle and Gloria could use (with illustration) will show children's understanding of the plot, the author-illustrator's use of humor in both text and pictures, and the readers' ability to extend this understanding to imagine new but similar situations.

Many times, ideas for activities arise from a story, almost as if they were embedded there waiting to be found. These frequently offer the most natural ways to engage with it. For example, children could closely examine David Diaz's illustrations in *Smoky Night* (1994) by Eve Bunting and discuss how the materials used in the collages match or interpret the text. Then students could create their own collages for sections of text with appropriate materials to show their interpretations. This activity accomplishes at least two worthwhile goals: It provides students with a better understanding of Diaz's artistic style and of why it complements the narrative so well, and it provides the teacher with knowledge about the students' interpretations of the story through that medium.

The key to maximizing young readers' involvement with activities is to provide options and variety. When they can make their own choices and have opportunities to express themselves in different modes, their imaginations can be stimulated and their ability to find relevance and meaning can be optimized. In addition, these activities should lead to deeper understanding of and engagement with the story; therefore, they should be meaningful, not trite. Teacher educator Nancy Roser's (2001) "What's Cute and What Counts?" test is a good way to distinguish between activities that are merely fun and those that are thoughtful (and also can be fun). I wanted my students to both *enjoy* responding to a text and respond *more deeply*. In short, I wanted them to learn something new about the story or literature in general from their own responses. Here is a partial list of ideas for response activities that I used with my students, some of them adapted from Reasoner (1976).

SAMPLE LITERATURE RESPONSE ACTIVITY IDEAS

1. Write a letter to a character in the book, telling what you think about his or her situation, actions, feelings, etc.

2. Write a letter from a character to a newspaper advice columnist, such as Abby, of "Dear Abby," about a problem or situation being faced. Write Abby's advice about what the character should do.
3. Write a letter from one character to another in the same or a different book telling her or his thoughts and feelings or making comparisons to the other character's situation.
4. Design an invitation to a character in a book. Make sure the event would be the kind of thing the character would want to do.
5. Design a wanted poster for any character in a book. Tell why the character is wanted and describe the character's looks, habits, and last known location.
6. Design buttons or T-shirts for the characters in a book. Make sure the slogans and logos fit the characters' personalities.
7. Draw TV or movie previews—four or five scenes—to advertise a book.
8. Write a newspaper account of an event in a book.
9. Write a diary for a character in a book.
10. Write the next episode that would happen after the end of the book.
11. Write time capsule predictions (5 or 10 years later) for the characters in a book. Tell what they would be doing and where they would be.
12. Write a telephone conversation between two characters in a book about the events or a situation in the book.

Note that many of these activities can be facilitated by access to computer word processing or graphic design programs that may be available in classrooms. Teachers can develop the activities electronically and have students complete them directly in the computer program rather than with conventional paper-and-pencil methods.

USING TEACHERS' GUIDES

Teachers' guides for children's books offer ideas for discussion questions and response activities that can be used when working with children. Many teachers appreciate the convenience of such guides, which often are created by publishers of the books or by teacher educators or consultants. However, I offer two cautions: Evaluate these guides carefully, using the considerations I've discussed above regarding questions and activities, and don't become overly dependent on any guides. (See children's literature consultant Susan Hepler's [1988] insightful critique of published guides, "Reading Between the Guide Lines.") As a teacher, I would examine the suggested questions and use any that I thought were open-ended and of a higher level, that stimulated *my* thinking, and that were developmentally appropriate for my students. Likewise, with the proposed activities, I would select those that were creative but meaningful, that led back into the story and encouraged a deeper involvement with it, and that were developmentally appropriate. I would avoid any activities that seemed superficial or only tangentially related to the story.

Many times teachers create their own, and the best, guides for the books they use in their teaching. (For a good discussion of how to create a guide for literary teaching, see Mary Lou Sorensen's [1995a] helpful model.) I have facilitated this effort by offering workshops for teachers where they can create guides and share them with each other. If they each develop a guide for a different book, they can quickly multiply their resources. A good example of one of these guides, created by Elisabeth Etzel for *The Well* (Taylor, 1995), is shown in Figure 3.2.

CREATING SMALL GROUPS

One important consideration to keep in mind is that, except for books that I read aloud and that everyone could enjoy regardless of reading proficiency, I never held literary discussions with the whole class. A single book will rarely, if ever, meet the needs and interests of everyone, and there are so many books from which to choose on similar themes or topics that there is no point in limiting children's reading to that extent. Furthermore, small groups are usually better for encouraging participation by everyone, rather than a confident or outspoken few, thus creating vital spaces for shared construction of meaning. Finally, since I can't be everywhere at once, children must learn to converse with each other about books, and the likelihood of their total dependence on my leadership (and my ideas about a book) is lessened.

My decision to use small groups means that I need to arrange those groups, which will depend on the purposes of the groups. If they are for readers to discuss a piece of literature based on their *interest*, then they will be grouped based on their selection. Such groups are likely to be heterogeneous. If, however, I see a particular *need* or developmental readiness to learn a particular concept, then I will group students based on my observations, and I will choose the material that we will use. Whatever the purpose, optimum small-group size is about four to seven children—large enough to generate sufficient ideas to stimulate thinking but small enough for everyone to participate easily. This can vary, though, depending on the age of the children and the number of groups a teacher can manage. Sometimes for activities such as reading aloud to each other, pairs or triads are best. Regardless of the configuration and purpose, all groups should be fluid and change regularly depending on the students' needs and interests. No child should remain in the same group(s) for indefinite periods of time. This kind of fluidity is better for children's development and removes any stigma that can become attached to a particular group.

Finally, individualization is important for both *literary* and *literacy* learning. Teachers need to offer choices about what to read and the opportunity for students to self-select based upon their interests. Children need time for uninterrupted reading and responding to books, and they need chances to share their responses with their peers and teachers. Independent reading helps students to practice their skill with reading, solidify their growth, pursue their interests, and refine their taste. This is the kind of reading in which they will most be engaged during the rest of their lives.

LITERATURE CIRCLES AND INSTRUCTIONAL GROUPS

As I stated regarding the purposes for groups, some are for interest and others are for identified needs. Literature circles, "discussion groups in which children meet regularly to talk about books" (Hill, Johnson, & Noe, 1995, p. 2), should be based upon interest. Children's literature and literacy expert Kathy Short (1999) clearly distinguishes between literature circles and instructional groups that are based on readers' needs and abilities and makes comparisons regarding the roles of students and teachers and the kinds of texts that are read in each type of group.

Literature circles are student selected based on students' interest in specific works selected from a choice of texts offered by the teacher or suggested by students. These heterogeneous groups are conducted by the group participants. Students may read the book for themselves or have it read to them by someone else. I participated in these groups on a rotating basis as a reader, and I modeled/demonstrated ways that I thought about and responded to the book. When a book is finished, the group may develop a culminating project together to share with the rest of the class, and then the group disbands. New groups are created for different books.

Instructional groups are generated on the basis of developmental needs and students' ability to read texts at about the same level of difficulty. Thus

Figure 3.2. Teacher's Guide: *The Well: David's Story.*
(Created by Elisabeth Etzel*)

Taylor, M. D. (1995). *The well: David's story.* New York: Dial Books for Young Readers.

Appropriate for ages 10–13.

Summary

David Logan is 10 the summer there is a drought in southern Mississippi. His family owns land with the only well that has not run dry. These African Americans share their water with all the families around them, both Black and White, despite existing racial tensions and some family opposition. David's mother feels that they have to share the gift that God has given them.

David and his older brother Hammer have trouble with their White neighbor boys, Charlie and Ed-Rose Simms, who treat them with blatant prejudice. David tries to follow his father's advice to use his head in dealing with White folks, but Hammer does not. He gets in trouble by smarting off and hitting Charlie. Eventually, the tension between Hammer and the Simms boys causes Charlie and Ed-Rose to poison the well. This action results in suffering for all the families around them.

Prereading Questions

1. How would you feel about sharing something you own with people who don't like you and don't treat you well?
2. How would you feel if one group of people looked down on you, ordered you around, and treated you meanly just for the way you look?
3. Look at the cover and title of this book. What do you think it will be about?

Postreading Questions

Read through the first line of p. 28 (Scholastic edition):

1. Taylor uses the word *nigger* in the book. This is a word that we should never use. Why do you think she includes it in the story?
2. Why do you think it bothered the Simmses that the Logans owned land and the well?

Read through p. 63 (Scholastic edition):

3. What do you think about Ma Rachel's behavior?

After finishing the book:

4. How do you think the Melbournes felt and why do you think they didn't ever get involved?
5. What do you think the poisoning of the well symbolized?
6. How did the way the Whites treated the Black people in this book make you feel?
7. Why do you think racial tension was such an issue at that time in history?

Activities

1. Create a Venn diagram comparing David and Hammer's reactions to the Simmses.
2. Draw a map of the Logan farm. Include key places such as their house, the well, the prayer rock, and so on.
3. Rewrite a scene in the book from Hammer's point of view.
4. Write a poem expressing the way that this book makes you feel.
5. Create an illustration of your favorite scene using the artistic medium of your choice.
6. Write a letter from Ma Logan to Pa Logan describing her thoughts about the events that took place between Charlie and Hammer while he was away.
7. Create a skit of what you think Hammer and Halton did while waiting at the prayer rock.

Other Books by Mildred D. Taylor about the Logan Family

(1975). *Song of the trees*. New York: Dial Press.

(1976). *Roll of thunder, hear my cry*. New York: Dial Press.

(1981). *Let the circle be unbroken*. New York: Dial Press.

(1987). *The friendship*. New York: Dial Books for Young Readers.

(1990). *Mississippi bridge*. New York: Dial Books for Young Readers.

(1990). *The road to Memphis*. New York: Dial Books.

(2001). *The land*. New York: Phyllis Fogelman Books.

---

* Elizabeth Etzel is a former graduate student at Ohio State University and currently an elementary classroom teacher.

THE IMPORTANCE OF LITERACY SKILLS INSTRUCTION—
AND LINKS TO LITERARY GROWTH

In *More Than Anything Else* (1995), Marie Bradby's picture book story about Booker T. Washington, Bradby vividly portrays his hunger to learn to read "more than anything else." When a young man teaches him how to "crack the code," Booker likens his feeling of joy to being baptized—or salvation, in essence. Thus the literacy skill he has acquired opens a whole new world of possibilities for literary learning and pleasure. In this chapter, I focus on the fact that readers (and writers) do not always simply develop organically in a literate environment. Certainly, being immersed in literature is fundamental, but there also are times when explicit attention needs to be paid to skills instruction in order for developing readers and writers to gain the tools they need to enjoy these activities. What I explore here is how to do that in a *literary* way.

Both the literary experience as defined by Louise Rosenblatt and the process of reading as described by Frank Smith are rooted in the constructivist model of learning that Jean Piaget developed. Thus, literature does not exist *out there* as an objectifiable work of art, but is created by a reader, on the basis of past experiences and present development, in transaction with a text. Likewise, reading is not an act of decoding marks on a printed page, but rather of a reader interacting with a text and using prior knowledge of the world and how texts work to construct meaning. Both literary and literacy experiences are essentially the same kind of processes, and many concepts for each are closely related or identical with different labels. In the following paragraphs, I explore some *literary* ideas and devices that have close corollaries in *literacy* concepts and instructional approaches.

1. One of these closely related conceptual pairs is *sense of story* and *comprehension*. Children develop a sense of story by being read or told many stories from a very young age. Narrative is a primary way for human beings to organize our experiences in the world, and "making sense of an experience is thus to a very great extent being able to construct a plausible story about it," according to researcher Gordon Wells (1986, p. 196). From the body of narratives that children hear, they develop a sense of what constitutes a story and, when listening to new ones, have "a set of expectations about how stories unfold" (Temple & Gillet, 1996, p. 132) and sound. Sense of story is essential for comprehension.

2. The set of expectations that is sense of story then becomes part of the prior knowledge that readers bring to stories. Children with a well-

developed sense of story "read and listen to stories with their expectations awakened; they read or listen actively, with their prior knowledge of stories assisting them in comprehending" (Temple & Gillet, 1996, p. 132). The way that prior knowledge assists comprehension is by enabling readers to make predictions (either consciously or unconsciously) about what will happen in the story based on their past experiences with texts. Making those connections is a result of intertextuality. Thus, *prior knowledge, prediction, and comprehension*—all literacy ideas—are closely aligned with *intertextuality*, or the "larger fabric of language and writing" (Moon, 1999, p. 93)—a literary understanding.

3. In addition, two specific literary devices—*foreshadowing* and *suspense*—may contribute to children's natural inclination to make *predictions* (Lehman, 1986). Children's literature expert Rebecca Lukens (2003) describes suspense as "a state that makes us read on" (p. 108). Cliff-hanger chapter endings are one common vehicle for adding suspense, while foreshadowing helps to balance suspense by creating a "sense of the inevitable" (p. 112). These devices invite children to guess or predict the next event or outcome of a story and make them want to read to discover if they are right.

4. Another literary-literacy pair is *themes* and *main ideas*. "Theme in literature is the idea that holds the story together . . . the main idea or central meaning of a piece of writing," explains Lukens (2003, p. 129). Main idea is described as a "central idea" and is included under "higher-order comprehension" in reading instruction, according to reading specialists Betty Roe, Sandy Smith, and Paul Burns (2005, p. 226). This deeper, underlying idea or "significant truth" remains with a reader "long after details of plot are forgotten" (Lukens, p. 130). These lasting meanings thus are the centerpiece of reading. In good literature, themes are not stated explicitly by the author (except as morals in fables), but are constructed by individual readers and are not precisely the same for different readers. (It's also worth reiterating here that construction of themes is culturally situated and may be contested by various readers.) Reference to "lessons" in a literary text is usually a more didactic (and less aesthetic) way of describing themes.

5. Along those same lines, *plot* and *sequence* carry some similar connotations, or at least sequence as the order of events in a story contributes to plot (Lukens, 2003). Plot is more than story sequence, however, as events may be arranged out of chronological order through flashbacks and other devices to achieve a particular effect. Teachers often check children's literal

comprehension of a story by asking them to engage in some type of se-quencing activity, such as story mapping or diagramming the plot. *Struc-ture* "refers to the way that the various parts of a text relate to one another and form patterns" (Nodelman & Reimer, 2003, p. 69) in a literary work, while similarly *story schema*—commonly discussed as a literacy con-cept—is a "mental representation of story structures, the elements that make up a story, and the way they are related" (Roe, Smith, & Burns, 2005, p. 205).

6. *Characterization* is the way that an author develops the characters in a story. It can be revealed by the portrayal of a character's actions, words, or thoughts; description of appearance; other characters' comments, thoughts, or actions toward the character; and what the author or narrator reveals about the character (Galda & Cullinan, 2006; Lukens, 2003). One mean-ingful way for children to explore characterization (and build literacy profi-ciency) is through *oral expression*, such as oral reading or dramatization, which allows readers to demonstrate their interpretation of how a character would speak and act.

7. An author's style of writing includes the "use of certain specific de-vices of *language*" (Lukens, 2003, p. 187, emphasis added), among which are denotative and connotative meanings of words, imagery, figurative lan-guage, and puns and wordplay. The literacy counterpart is *vocabulary*, which includes all of the above, and is essential to comprehension. For example, puns and wordplay often are created through multiple meanings, homonyms, and idioms; imagery is portrayed through concrete adjectives, nouns, and verbs. Furthermore, researcher Carol Chomsky (1972) shows that children's language development seems to have direct correlation with their exposure to a wide variety of rich literature.

CLOSING THE LITERARY-LITERACY GAP

As noted above, exposure to rich children's books offers many benefits for both literary and literacy development. In this section, I describe examples of specific teaching methods that can accomplish important goals in both areas. They are not, however, intended to be a comprehensive "scope and sequence" of literary-literacy instruction, but rather suggestions that I hope will make clear how this kind of teaching happens and that provide teachers with a starting point for developing their own ideas.

Enhancing Literary Development Through Literacy Instruction

Sense of Story

I have already stated that sense of story is developed through hearing many stories from a very young age (probably birth). Children who have such experiences develop a much stronger sense of story than those who don't have those opportunities, and story sense lays a solid foundation for reading achievement. Hence, it is especially critical for teachers to immerse students who may not have had this advantage before school in a rich storying environment, and *all* children will benefit. In addition to hearing stories, children can grow by retelling stories that they have heard to each other and to adults, such as teachers or parents. I had my students retell stories orally with puppets, flannel board cutouts, or other pictures; dramatization; or in writing. This is also a perfect opportunity for children to tell stories that were told to them by their families and members of their communities, thus bringing and honoring their home cultures in school. All these activities were occasions for me to observe and nurture their growing sense of story.

Story Language

Stories sound a certain way, often with conventional beginnings and endings and the typical use of past tense. In addition, certain sentence structures and words are much more likely to be encountered in written language than in speech. Hearing folktales, especially, helps children to develop an understanding of story language. These stories often begin with "Once upon a time," "There was a time," or "It happened." They may end with "And they lived happily ever after," "The teller is tired. The story is done," or "Snip, snap, snout. This tale's told out." The action in a story may be advanced with a sentence beginning with "And so it came about" or "Some time later." I would learn about and encourage my students' sense of story language by having them retell stories or compose original ones. Examining the kind of language, sentence structures, and story conventions they used gave me a good idea of their knowledge of how stories often sound. Children of all language abilities and backgrounds can benefit from this practice.

Structure/Narrative Progression

As already noted, children's understanding of plot structures and narrative progression directly affects their comprehension. Useful literacy techniques that promote these understandings involve creating various styles of story maps or diagrams. For example, one common narrative structure is the circle story, in which the hero sets out from home, has one or more adventures, and returns safely home (usually changed in some way) in the end. This is easily demonstrated with picture books (such as *The Story About Ping*, Flack, 1933; *Sylvester and the Magic Pebble*, Steig, 1969; or *Down the Road*, Schertle, 1995) and folktales (such as "Jack and the Beanstalk," "Hansel and Gretel," or the Eritrean tale *Trouble*, Kurtz, 1997). (See annotations in Children's Books Cited.) In addition, the circle motif appears in much literature for older children, especially quest fantasies, such as *A Wrinkle in Time* (L'Engle, 1962), and also contemporary stories, such as Beverley Naidoo's *Journey to Jo'burg* (1985). Reading several circle stories to children and having them illustrate the episodes of the hero's adventure in a circle diagram helps young readers to understand this narrative structure and to recognize when they encounter it in new stories. They also can invent circle stories in their own writing. Children, including English-language learners, who cannot write stories themselves can dictate their narratives to an adult or more capable peer.

Prior Literary Knowledge

Literary understanding—such as how to distinguish genres, what typically happens to a protagonist, how plots unfold, what kind of settings to expect with certain genres (such as fantasy, folklore, or realistic fiction), and what to expect from familiar authors or about favorite characters—contributes to readers' store of prior knowledge. This, in turn, enhances their ability to make predictions and develop good comprehension. One useful method that activates readers' prior knowledge is the directed reading (or listening)-thinking activity (DRTA/DLTA), developed by literacy educator Russell Stauffer (1969). The basic premise of this problem-solving technique is to involve children in thinking actively about what they are reading or hearing. They ask questions or make hypotheses about what will happen in a story and then read or listen to find out if they were right. Twice, when children make their predictions and then when they evaluate their findings, teachers should ask them to give reasons. With children, we should use developmentally appropriate literary terminology and encourage them to make and evaluate predictions based on their prior literary knowledge.

　　For example, with younger children, regarding a new story by a favorite author, I can ask them what kind (genre) of story they think the one we are reading is and where and when they think it will take place (setting). If the story is a folktale, I can ask children to predict how the plot will develop based on their knowledge of other folktales (intertextuality). For older readers, I might have readers defend their predictions based on their knowledge of characterization and what likely happens to a protagonist in a quest story, for example. If there are foreshadowing devices, I can note those points and ask readers to make and defend predictions based on these clues. These kinds of questions require children to go beyond simple sequential (or what happens next) thinking to a more analytical stance involving background literary knowledge. Thus a literacy technique can help to strengthen young readers' ability to actively employ a growing repertoire of tools for creating meaning from literary texts. Because it works equally well as both a listening *and* reading exercise, this strategy promotes the literary development of children with all abilities.

Characterization, Point of View, and Role of the Narrator

I've already noted that oral reading and dramatization can help children gain a better understanding of characterization; they also enhance insights about the role of the narrator. Readers' theater is one enjoyable and meaningful way to engage in oral reading and to develop fluency and expression, which is important for all readers and particularly supportive for struggling readers or English-language learners. This technique involves transforming a story or book chapter from its original form into a script that can be read or even dramatized. In this process, children change the text so that a narrator delivers any material not spoken by a character. They also can explore the differences and similarities between the narrator and the author and can determine from what point of view the story is told. When the script is read or performed, readers dramatize the characters through vocal expression of their interpretations of the characters' personalities. Another method I used for engaging children in meaningful oral reading was having my students read books aloud to other children, either one reading to another in buddy pairs or an older student reading to groups of younger children—a great confidence builder for children whose reading proficiency may be lagging behind their peers'. These activities build fluency skill and develop interpretive expression.

Themes

Developing open-ended questions to guide literary discussions about the main ideas of a story or offering appropriate, creative activities to encourage children's expression of and interaction with those ideas are two ways to nurture young readers' understanding of themes. I've already described how to develop these questions and activities in Chapter 3, but here I describe several ideas for a specific book, *Rose Blanche*, by Christophe Gallaz and Roberto Innocenti (1985). (See annotation in Children's Books Cited.)

One of the most intriguing aspects of this story is the perspective shift from first person to omniscient about halfway through the story after Rose Blanche discovers the camp. Why does this happen, I want to know? What might be the purpose of this perspective shift, and how does it contribute to theme? I believe that Rose Blanche portrays innocence or perhaps more accurately lack of understanding. She never asks her mother questions about the camp she has discovered (something we would expect a typically curious child to do), perhaps symbolizing the world's lack of recognition of what was going on in the Holocaust and unwillingness to ask questions to find out. When she finds the camp and the perspective shifts from her voice to that of the narrator, is this because she has lost her "voice" as an innocent child? Is she now aware that asking questions would be too dangerous?

I'm also intrigued by her name, which means "rose white" in French and reminds me of the Grimms' fairy tale "Snow White and Rose Red" and is a merging of two names into one. What connections, if any, might there be with this story? For example, in both stories a child/children walk into a forest and make a discovery. Is this symbolically significant? Yet another point I would discuss with children is why the story begins in winter and ends in spring, as explicitly noted on the first and last pages of text. What does this mean, and why is it spring (a season that typically signifies hope) when Rose Blanche disappears, an event I regard with sadness and irony? I want children to contemplate these ideas with me and recognize that when others aren't willing to recognize the truth, courage (even if it means death) finally results in hope being restored.

For an activity, I would pair this book with *Star of Fear, Star of Hope* (Hoestlandt, 1993), a story in which Helen, now a grandmother, recalls the treatment of her Jewish friend under the Nazi occupation of France. (See annotation in Children's Books Cited.) There are intriguing thematic similarities and differences between these two books, and one way to highlight those would be first to discuss Helen's underlying message to readers. Then ask children who have heard both stories to imagine that Rose Blanche also lived to be an old woman. If she could write a message that she wanted the world to know, like Helen, what might hers be? How would it compare to Helen's message? Students can write imaginary messages from Rose Blanche and compare their messages with each other's and with what we thought was Helen's. In this way, they can see that themes can be perceived and stated differently by various readers.

Language Appreciation

One of the best ways for children to gain appreciation for language and expand their vocabulary knowledge is through hearing and reading books with rich examples of language. William Steig's *Amos and Boris* (1971) is one excellent source for developing language appreciation. In this story about the friendship between a "mote of a mouse" and a "mountain of a whale," a story in which each rescues the other in a time of crisis, we encounter such rich, descriptive language as "a phosphorescent sea," "whales spouting luminous water," and "thoroughly akin to it all." These examples may not represent the typical vocabulary of children who are at the age at which they would enjoy this lovely tale. However, they can savor the beautiful sounds of the words, and they can probably deduce enough of what the words mean from the contexts in which they are used to enjoy their contribution to the story's imagery. Finally, after hearing the story, we can return to these words or others that the listeners find puzzling and discuss what the children think they mean and compare their ideas to the actual meanings. Doing this increases children's interest in words and their confidence in their ability to figure out unknown meanings, an important step toward reading independence for all children.

Poetry is another source of rich language that is playful, sensory stimulating, and highly symbolic—certainly a large part of Dr. Seuss's appeal is his playful verse containing coined words. J. Patrick Lewis creates clever puns with his poetry, as in the title of *Good Mousekeeping* (2001), a collection that includes a flamingo that lives in a "flamingolow" or a cat in "THE COTTAGE CHEESE" (unpaginated). The subject of the entire collection of Nikki Grimes's (2001) *A Pocketful of Poems* is about words and the connotations that they evoke. *FEG: Ridiculous ~~Stupid~~ Poems for Intelligent Children* by Robin Hirsch (2002) is a celebration of poetic wordplay and puns, such as the various meanings of *flush*—all accompanied by footnotes containing witty but informative explanations of language terms used. Poetry can introduce different dialects of English and other languages, sometimes embedded within English-language poems and sometimes in parallel language versions. Katharine Boling's *New Year Be Coming! A Gullah Year* (2002) captures the speech rhythms and sounds of the Gullah patois in poems linked to the months of the year. The nursery rhymes in *No Hickory, No Dickory, No Dock* (1995) bounce with the dialects of authors John Agard and Grace Nichols's native

Caribbean. Pat Mora's poems in *Confetti* (1996) are liberally sprinkled with Spanish, her mother tongue, while the same poems for the 2006 translation are presented entirely in Spanish (2006). (See Children's Books Cited for annotations.) This is just a sampling of methods that I have found to promote literary development through literacy instruction.

Contributions of Literature to Literacy Development

Now I turn to several appropriate ways that literature can contribute to literacy development (and that have been extensively covered elsewhere in the professional literature).

Elaborated Oral Language

One of the traits that young children need as they emerge into literacy is a strong basis in oral language. Children with more elaborated oral language will have a better foundation for learning to read and write. This includes understanding of word meanings (semantics) and of grammatical forms (syntax) and the ability to use these for thinking (Gillet, Temple, & Crawford, 2004). Listening to many stories and hearing them multiple times are important ways to promote all children's elaborated language, because well-written books are one of the best sources of such language, as I've already described above. Listening to language used in meaningful contexts, such as stories, helps children from other language backgrounds to learn English. Discussing these stories also promotes oral language fluency for all children.

Concepts About Print

Literacy researcher Marie Clay (1979) identified these concepts as, among others, book orientation, the directionality of print on a page, the understanding that print (not the picture) is read, knowledge of alphabet letters and simple punctuation, and understanding of reading terminology such as *letter* and *word*. All these concepts can be developed by children as they watch adults model handling and reading books and through their being allowed to handle many books themselves. One specific strategy that effectively and naturally highlights these concepts is the shared book experience originated in New Zealand by Don Holdaway (1979). In this method, a teacher reads aloud an enlarged version of a storybook to a group of emergent readers. The children watch as the adult points out and discusses features of print, such as those noted above, and learn key literacy terminology, such as the names of common punctuation marks, in the context of immediate use.

Details

Remembering explicit details, an aspect of literal comprehension, is not the most important element of reading, but details do contain information on which higher-level comprehension rests. Thus if enough details are missed, deeper understandings may suffer. One effective and appropriate way to encourage the use of details for thinking is having children offer proof that their predictions in a DRTA or DLTA are or are not probable or correct. Similarly, in making predictions, children can be detail sleuths, searching for clues about what will happen next in the story being read. As in the research finding I described in Chapter 1, young children frequently are expert at close observation, as was Caleb in *Sarah, Plain and Tall* (MacLachlan, 1985), who noticed that Sarah did not take her cat with her when she left to drive into town alone and thus predicted that she would return to the family.

Alphabet Knowledge

Knowledge of letter names and features and what letters do (serve as signs representing spoken sounds) are all aspects of alphabet knowledge, an important precursor of beginning reading. Many good alphabet books provide children with opportunities to explore all these aspects of alphabet knowledge. They also draw attention to beginning sounds of words, since each letter of the alphabet usually is represented by one or more words that begin with that letter. This distinction of beginning sounds of words is the foundation for phonological awareness.

Phonological and Phonemic Awareness

Phonological awareness is recognition of sounds in oral language, while phonemic awareness is more specifically the perception of units of sound from which words are built. These concepts are essential for emergent literacy, and they can be developed through poetry and its rhyming and alliteration. These poetic devices help children with two key ingredients for phonemic awareness: onsets (the beginning sounds of words or syllables) and rimes (the part that follows from the vowel to the end of the word or syllable). Choral reading or speaking of favorite nursery rhymes or poems is a highly effective way to promote this awareness and discrimination (and also provides a very supportive context for less able readers and English-language learners). Many picture books contain such rhymes and poetry, and they can be displayed on large chart paper for a group to read together. Then the teacher can print lists of the rhyming words and of the words that begin with the same letter/ sound to show children what letters make these onsets and rimes.

Sight Words and Word Study

Sight words, or words recognized immediately, are the "stepping stones" that help emergent readers to progress through a line of print that contains other unknown words (Gillet, Temple, & Crawford, 2004, p. 228). It is important for a reader to have enough of these to successfully negotiate text, just as it would be critical for a hiker to have enough stepping-stones on which to cross a stream without falling in the water. If a reader has enough sight words, he or she can use context to figure out the remaining unknown words. Sight words are gained from any source, even a sign or logo, that is interesting and meaningful to a child. They also are acquired from children's books, especially ones that use interesting, predictable, patterned language and repetition, such as *Feathers for Lunch* (Ehlert, 1990) or *Where Once There Was a Wood* (Fleming, 1996). (See annotations in Children's Books Cited.) Many books like these make good candidates for class-made big books or already are produced commercially in enlarged format to be used in shared book experiences. Reading them, or any favorite books, repeatedly makes their text and individual words memorable and eventually recognizable on sight. These words become the basis for word study, or the process of analyzing words to establish patterns that then can be applied by analogy to new, unknown words. Through word study (also referred to as analytic phonics [Gillet, Temple, & Crawford, 2004]), children add to their word knowledge and decoding strategies, their store of sight words, and their growing independence as readers. (More specific information about word-study activities, such as word sorts, may be found in Gillet, Temple, and Crawford, 2004, or other sources.) Becoming increasingly adept and knowledgeable about words enhances all readers' fluency and enjoyment with reading literature.

Visual Discrimination

This skill is often included in literacy curricula, and it is naturally developed through viewing pictures in children's books. Illustrations are often artistically excellent and visually stimulating; for examples, see any of Thomas Locker's books (such as *Water Dance*, 1997; *Cloud Dance*, 2000; or *Moun-*

tain Dance, 2001) with their beautifully executed oil landscape paintings, or Paul Zelinsky's exquisite and fitting Italian Renaissance–style art in his retelling of *Rapunzel* (1997). Many picture books satisfy young children's fascination with examining illustrations for extensive periods of time, but some are particularly challenging, such as Graeme Base's highly inventive alphabet book, *Animalia* (1987), with its richly layered puzzles for each letter over which to pore for hours. Walter Wick also is a master at creating picture puzzles, such as those in *Can You See What I See?* (2002), a series of visual problems and illusions produced by photographing arrangements of real objects. Likewise, in *Backyard Detective: Critters Up Close* (2002), Nic Bishop has developed astonishing photographic collages showing life-size animal habitats that invite young readers to discover the 125 "critters" portrayed (and sometimes cleverly disguised) and that lead to exciting science inquiry. For cross-cultural artistic connections, Niki Daly's dramatic paintings for his and Nola Turkington's story, *The Dancer* (1996), borrow from the San style of rock art to bring this southern African story to life. Readers of all ability levels can enjoy and benefit from viewing illustrations closely.

Writing and Composing

As noted repeatedly in this chapter, much children's literature is a superb source of well-crafted language. By paying attention to the way that stories are written, students can gain appreciation for what authors do and form a stronger identity of themselves as writers. One valuable exercise that I had my students try was writing a picture book in the style of one of their favorite stories from when they were younger. In this manner, one of my fourth graders borrowed from Mercer Mayer's *There's a Nightmare in My Closet* (1968) to create her version of "There's a Monster Under My Bed." More subtly, students can examine authors' use of description, imagery, or dialogue, for example, or unique narrative structures, such as in Lonnie's story about the loss of his parents and his living in a foster home away from his sister, all told through a series of his poems in *Locomotion*, by Jacqueline Woodson (2003), as described in Chapter 3 (Figure 3.1). Children's literature can make an important contribution, therefore, to the development of young writers as models of excellent writing and inspiration for their compositions.

There are numerous other teaching ideas in the professional literature that involve children's literature in literacy instruction. The examples presented here are some that I have found to be effective and appropriate and that do not violate literary integrity.

THE PLACE OF BASAL READERS AND OTHER TEXTBOOKS
IN A LITERARY CLASSROOM

Basal reading programs and other textbooks have many well-documented shortcomings (see, for example, Goodman, Shannon, Freeman, & Murphy, 1988; Moss, 1991; and Woodward, Elliott, & Nagel, 1986), and educators have long called for the use of more children's literature and less, if any, use of textbooks and basals. However, many elementary teachers are stuck with required materials such as these. I was one of these teachers, although I found ways to use them selectively and not necessarily in the prescribed sequence. Rather, I used my students' needs to guide my selection and use of material and chose the best suggested practices and questions from the teacher's manual. Mostly, I developed my own higher-level questions and creative, meaningful learning experiences for the stories we read. Further, I linked basal selections to the whole texts from which they were taken and to other related literature, thus making the basal reader one more entry into the literary world.

Basal readers, if evaluated carefully, can be a useful source of multiple copies of short stories or book passages keyed to reading levels for use in guided-reading groups. Recall that in these settings the members are of homogeneous ability and it is important to use material that is at their instructional reading level. Other textbooks can be used as resources (along with many other written materials and books) that provide breadth (but usually not depth) of information. This basic information can help to introduce or summarize various topics of study. Such resources also may contain informative graphics, maps, photos, illustrations, definitions of specialized terminology, and bibliographies for further investigation. Under a thoughtful, knowledgeable teacher, these materials can be used wisely. However, basal programs and other textbooks generally should be minimized as much as possible; instead, students should have as many opportunities as possible in school to read from the wealth of excellent fiction and nonfiction available today.

Children's literature does have an important place in the curriculum, not for literary study in isolation, but simultaneously with skills instruction. Teachers, who have a strong understanding of literature and its theory, about literacy principles and processes, and about connections between the two will be able to help their students grow in both ways at the same time. Skillful readers and writers will enjoy the pleasures of literary engagements even more. In the following chapter, I explore how to extend and enhance literary study across the curriculum.

5

Literary Learning and the Whole Curriculum

A S I DID WITH my fourth graders, I read aloud frequently to my undergraduate and graduate students, who are either preparing to become or already are elementary and middle school teachers. These pre- and in-service teachers typically are enthusiastic about the possibilities that literature holds for enriching learning experiences in a wide variety of subjects, and they often approach a new book for the lessons that they can derive from it for their teaching. For example, when I read aloud a book such as *Amos & Boris* (Steig, 1971), it's not uncommon for my listeners to zero in almost at once on the potential for using the book to launch a study of mammals. However, this story also offers a wealth of opportunities for literary study. In earlier chapters, I've noted its exquisite use of language, but it also has powerful themes, including how friends can help each other, regardless of size; having a sense of adventure and taking risks; and taking the time to enjoy life. Thus, while I *might* include this title in a science unit on mammals, I certainly would focus students' attention first on its literary qualities. The same could be true of much excellent nonfiction I would include in such a unit.

Literary learning, then, does not end with the literacy curriculum (which I've discussed in the previous two chapters), but should extend to the whole curriculum as part of a comprehensive structure for literary study. Furthermore, "whole literature" includes both fiction and literary nonfiction as "two ways of knowing literature" (Crook & Lehman, 1991, p. 35), and intertextuality applies not just to texts but to learning as a whole. Thus, literary learning is part of holistic learning that is enhanced by "as many different types of discourse as applicable" (Sloan, 2003, p. 176), including informational books, folklore, poetry, and fiction.

Indeed, some theories of nonfiction, such as Jo Carr's (1982), emphasize that "the literature of fact" not only stimulates the intellect, but also leads to "awakened understanding" (p. 4), provides "imaginative interpretation" (p. 6), and instills passion. Wells (1986) proposes that facts (as found in nonfiction) "take on significance when they are related to other facts, and connections of various kinds made between them" (p. 204)—in other words, they constitute a theory or "macro-narrative" (p. 205) that involves imaginative thinking. This type of thinking is a powerful resource in all areas of learning. Langer (1995) describes several different ways for literary thinking across the curriculum: using story to connect abstract principles to students' lives (providing relevance), as motivation for learning about a topic, and using "a present-day scenario to consider What if . . . ?" (p. 135) in problem solving.

LITERARY QUALITIES IN NONFICTION

One of the ways to clarify literary thinking across the curriculum might be to examine some of the literary traits that can be found in informational books (and extended with other genres) (adapted from Freeman, Lehman, & Scharer, 1995).

Metaphor

I begin with *metaphor* (see Appendix A: Glossary of Literary Terms for definitions of all literary terms used in this chapter). *Flight* is an example of symbolic thinking that has strong connections with history, social studies, science, and literary-mythical understandings. There have been many occasions for people to flee persecution and war, both historically and currently—African slaves fleeing from the Southern United States to freedom in the North, Jews fleeing the Holocaust, refugees fleeing despotic regimes in Haiti or El Salvador, and Sudanese ethnic groups fleeing genocide in Darfur, to name a few. These should be studied in social studies and history classes, and the thematic implications of escape from oppression can be reinforced with Virginia Hamilton's *The People Could Fly* (1985, 2004), a folktale about Black slaves in the United States who flew up in the air to freedom, and her factual *Many Thousand Gone: African Americans from Slavery to Freedom* (1993). The flight migration patterns of birds interest scientists, environmentalists, and (with the spread of bird flu) medical epidemiologists. A good text about this phenomenon is *Hawk Highway in the Sky: Watching Raptor Migration* (1997) by Caroline Arnold and with full-color photographs by Robert Kruidenier. Birds' ability to fly was closely studied by inventors, who eventually mastered the physics for aircraft. Several biographies of the Wright brothers are available for young readers, but *To Fly: The Story of the Wright Brothers* (Old, 2002) particularly highlights their fascination with flight. *First to Fly: How Wilbur and Orville Wright Invented the Airplane*, by Peter Busby (2002), explores the science of flying in detail. Human flight has captured the imagination of storytellers at least since the time of the ancient Greeks and the myth of Icarus. Arthur Yorinks and Richard Egielski put a modern spin on this motif in the Caldecott Award winner *Hey, Al* (1986). (See annotations in Children's Books Cited.)

Another way to illustrate the literary cross-curricular links is to use one book—*Flight*—to explore this metaphor. Charles Lindbergh's famous trans-atlantic flight is depicted vividly in Robert Burleigh's (1991) picture book biographical account. The narrative embodies Lindbergh as the archetypal hero: brave, daring, and overcoming harrowing odds that could have led to disaster. He wasn't always a hero, though, but was initially unknown. The first and last sentence, "It is 1927, and his name is Charles Lindbergh" (unpaginated), is identical but serves completely different purposes. At the beginning, it is an introduction to this unknown man, who otherwise remains nameless throughout the story. At the end, both the date and name are now famous. Lindbergh's heroism contrasts intriguingly with his youthfulness and vulnerability, as presented in the illustrations (particularly the last one, in which the "hero" ironically is sprawled on a bed asleep) and by his stated age of 25. The story also portrays a sense of isolation and solitude through the lonely flight across the dark ocean, as Lindburgh fought sleep, hunger, fog, and ice: "He feels completely alone in the world" (unpaginated). These two concepts—heroism and loneliness—can be explored. How are they interrelated? How do they interact with the metaphor of *flight*? For older readers, further investigation of Lindbergh's now-tarnished image as a Nazi sympathizer would add interesting complications to the heroic iconography presented in this book. Also, his freedom to *choose* to fly can be contrasted with how slaves who were caught fleeing were severely punished and how even migrating birds fly to survive, not out of choice.

In other curricular links, the art of the illustrations in *Flight* can be studied. How does the artist use perspective to enhance the literary qualities discussed above? The opening double-page illustration, for example—a view of Lindbergh's airplane from ground level between his spread legs—accentuates his larger-than-life, soon-to-be heroic image. Throughout the book, color is used to enhance mood and themes: dark, cold colors reflect "the other side of midnight, the loneliest hours" (unpaginated), while morning and the sighting of land are accompanied by the bright hues of hope. A time line (bringing in math) of the 33½-hour flight could be developed to gain a better understanding of how repeatedly stating the passage of time builds suspense in the narrative. Locating Lindbergh's flight on a map (geography) can enhance readers' sense of place, or setting, and the vast distance he had to cover alone.

Setting

Depictions of *setting* can be explored further through other excellent informational books. Diane Swanson's award-winning *Safari Beneath the Sea: The Wonder World of the North Pacific Coast* (1994) reveals the setting in its title. Another unique ecosystem is portrayed in *Everglades* (1995) by Jean Craighead George. Wendell Minor's rich paintings beautifully show the evolution of this endangered setting. Similarly, Lynne Cherry's *A River Ran Wild: An Environmental History* (1992) recounts 6 centuries of history about the changes in the once-pure Nashua River running through what is now New Hampshire and Massachusetts. Joseph Bruchac's *Between Earth and Sky: Legends of Native American Sacred Places* (1996) poetically evokes traditional accounts of settings across North America that are gorgeously portrayed in Thomas Locker's oil landscape paintings. One of these sacred places, the Grand Canyon, is singled out in Wendell Minor's *Grand Canyon: Exploring a Natural Wonder* (1998), in which Minor studies this awesome setting from many perspectives in dramatic watercolor paintings. The presentations of this setting can be compared in these two books. Joys and traditions of the Christmas holidays are celebrated in two contrasting settings on a Virginia plantation just before the Civil War in Patricia and Fredrick McKissack's *Christmas in the Big House, Christmas in the Quarters* (1994). John Thompson's full-page acrylic paintings in rich, warm colors illustrate the master's Big House and the slaves' quarters. Finally, *Ogbo: Sharing Life in an African Village* (1996) by Ifeoma Onyefulu transports readers beyond our national borders to the less familiar but contemporary setting of Nigeria. The author's color photographs show a vibrant, close-knit village, and her text explains the inhabitants' communal way of life.

Point of View

Another literary element—*point of view*—also can be explored in nonfiction. All the Magic School Bus books, for example, *The Magic School Bus Inside the Human Body* (1989), by Joanna Cole, present the text from multiple points of view: the main narrative line from the collective viewpoint of

Ms. Frizzle's students, bubble quotes from various characters, and labels and student reports from an objective point of view. In addition, Bruce Degen's humorous illustrations depict the additional layer of visual perspective from an imaginary journey inside the human body. Synthesizing all the viewpoints requires considerable interaction on the part of readers, which can be facilitated by discussion focusing on these qualities.

History can sometimes be illuminated in new ways by examining events from new points of view. For example, Julius Lester uses an authorial voice in *From Slave Ship to Freedom Road* (1998) and directly addresses readers. Furthermore, he presents separate "imagination exercises" for White and African American readers—asking Whites to imagine a slave's perspective, Blacks to face their slavery history, and both to take the unsavory perspective of an aggressor. The provocative text, inspired by Rod Brown's disturbing paintings, "ask[s] us to step out of our skins and put on the skins of others" (unpaginated), thereby gaining empathy for others' experiences. Another book that requires readers to consider history from a perspective other than the dominant one is *Squanto's Journey: The Story of the First Thanksgiving* (2000), by Joseph Bruchac. In this account, our national myth is told from the first-person viewpoint of Squanto, the Patuxet Indian who befriended the English Pilgrims, a side of the story not often told. This perspective contrasts with Jean Craighead George's *The First Thanksgiving* (1993), a more standard omniscient account that also casts Squanto as the hero. Even the covers of these two books capture their different perspectives: Squanto appears in the foreground with the *Mayflower* sailing in the background in Greg Shed's illustration for the Bruchac (2000) work, while the Pilgrims stand in front with Indians approaching from the distance in Thomas Locker's painting for George's (1993) book. Although both books present Squanto heroically, the different points of view from which they do that possibly reveal differences in the authors' ideologies.

Sometimes information can be conveyed and enlivened from an inanimate object's point of view, such as in Faith Ringgold's *If a Bus Could Talk: The Story of Rosa Parks* (1999), in which, as the title states, the civil rights hero's fateful ride is recounted by a personified bus to a fictional girl on her way to school. Likewise, in *Call Me Ahnighito* (1995), by Pam Conrad, a meteorite discovered in Greenland and christened Ahnighito tells its own story of being found by Robert Peary's expedition in 1897 and brought to the American Museum of Natural History in New York. Finally, Peter Sís's masterpiece, *Tibet Through the Red Box* (1998), reconstructs the period in the author's life when his father, a filmmaker, was lost in Tibet for several years, through two points of view: his own as an adult recounting childhood memories and his father's through a diary kept during the Tibet wanderings. Older readers will enjoy the challenge of unifying the separate threads presented in text passages, in different fonts, and the magical, dreamlike illustrations.

Theme

Themes are abundant in literary nonfiction. One that works very naturally across the curriculum *and* across literary genres is the importance of cycles in all of life (this discussion is adapted from Crook and Lehman, 1991). Such a thematic exploration might begin with a novel, such as *Tuck Everlasting* (1975), by Natalie Babbitt, in which young Winnie happens upon a magical spring in a woods near her home that, unbeknownst to her, can give a person who drinks from it everlasting life. This theme—the enticement and tragedy of living forever—is reinforced by a Ferris wheel, symbolizing how life is a cycle, of which dying is a part, that never stops turning. Readers who are at the age at which they begin to understand death may find the prospect of never dying to be fascinating and desirable, but this book will help them to contemplate the sobering consequences of such an outcome, just as the Tucks help Winnie to do. Other life cycles can be explored in nonfiction such as Patricia Lauber's *Volcano: The Eruption and Healing of Mount St. Helens* (1986), which portrays the cycle of destruction and rebirth that happens when a volcano erupts, or *Pumpkin Circle* (1999), by George Levenson, about the life cycle of pumpkins.

Closely aligned with many plant cycles is the yearly cycle of seasons. *Ox-Cart Man* (1979) by Donald Hall portrays the yearly cycle of a New England pioneer family's life through lyrical text and Barbara Cooney's Caldecott Award–winning illustrations. American Indians' lives also were closely linked with nature's seasons, as exemplified through poetry in *Thirteen Moons on Turtle's Back: A Native American Year of Moons* (1992) by Joseph Bruchac and Jonathan London. Thomas Locker's collaboration with Candace Christiansen in *Sky Tree: Seeing Science Through Art* (1995) is a visual and scientific celebration of seasons and weather as depicted through the changes of a lone tree throughout a year's cycle.

Weather cycles make a natural next link, particularly the rising and fading pattern of storms. Books such as Franklyn Branley's *Flash, Crash, Rumble, and Roll* (1985) and *Tornado Alert* (1988) offer basic information for young readers about the formation and passing of these storms. Other titles for older readers focus on the worst hurricanes of the 20th century—in *Hurricanes: Earth's Mightiest Storms* (1996), by Patricia Lauber—and the blizzard of 1888 that paralyzed the northeastern United States in Jim Murphy's

Blizzard: The Storm That Changed America (2000). Robert McCloskey's Caldecott Award–winning *Time of Wonder* (1957), the story of one beautiful and awesome late-summer storm on an island off the coast of Maine, remains a classic.

Finally, children can explore mathematical cycles, such as the patterns found in how we mark the yearly recurring passage of time: 4 seasons, 12 months, 52 weeks, 365 days. Subdivide these further into 7 days in a week, 24 hours in a day, 60 minutes in an hour, and so forth. A book such as *Me Counting Time: From Seconds to Centuries* (2000), by Joan Sweeney, depicts these concepts in a lighthearted way. Another numerical cycle is our base 10 number system, and counting by exponents of 10 to represent exponential numbers is portrayed in David Schwartz's *On Beyond a Million: An Amazing Math Journey* (1999). A third numerical cycle is found in doubling, and *One Grain of Rice: A Mathematical Folktale* (1997), Demi's retelling of a fable from India, demonstrates how, by doubling, one grain of rice multiplies into more than a billion in just 30 days.

This extended exploration of one theme should demonstrate that good nonfiction contains many literary values that can be experienced throughout the curriculum. There are plenty of other topics as well, such as survival or journeys or ecology, which have strong cross-curricular links and literary potential to develop into full thematic studies.

THEMATIC UNITS

The previous discussion of the importance of cycles in all of life exemplifies what elementary teacher Peggy Oxley (1995) describes as a "literary tapestry" (p. 214), or how one theme can evolve into another, such as in the subthemes I describe above. Her integrated primary curriculum weaves together one thread with another and another, helping her second-graders to see the interrelationships between subjects as part of the universal whole we call life. Thematic units centered on unifying concepts can make these linkages clear.

It's important to clarify a distinction at this point. As noted by teacher educators Keith Barton and Lynne Smith (2000), a "serious shortcoming" of so-called thematic units is that they often "do not truly focus on a theme, but instead revolve around what might be called instructional motifs" (p. 55) such as "apples," or what I call topics. The difference between topics and themes is that a topic can be expressed in one word, such as *cycles*—to use the example I described in the previous section. A theme, by contrast, says something about that topic, such as "the importance of cycles in all of life," or even more fully as "cycles are an important way to describe many aspects of nature and patterns for organizing all of life." The problem with a topic is that it doesn't supply much substance or coherence to a unit of study. Instead, the topic is simply a superficial "vehicle for practicing unrelated . . . skills" (p. 55).

Thus, a topic such as survival, which I suggested above, would need to be developed into an idea or statement *about* survival, such as "survival is a basic drive for all living things." Then we could explore this theme from many different perspectives: for example, the rehabilitation and care of sick and injured animals in *Wildlife Rescue: The Work of Dr. Kathleen Ramsay* (1994), by Jennifer Dewey; how children helped their families survive by undertaking dangerous, arduous jobs in *Kids at Work: Lewis Hine and the Crusade Against Child Labor* (1994), by Russell Freedman; the survival of Jewish children during the Holocaust in convents, orphanages, and non-Jewish homes in Howard Greenfeld's *Hidden Children* (1993); the survival of both American bison and the Comanche Indian culture in Neil Waldman's *They Came from the Bronx: How the Buffalo Were Saved from Extinction* (2001); and how children and their families survive living in a garbage dump in Guatemala City in *Out of the Dump: Writings and Photographs by Children from Guatemala* (1995), edited by Kristine Franklin and Nancy McGirr. Thus, choosing an appropriate theme and wording it to represent a fundamental idea or "enduring question" (Valencia & Lipson, 1998) is a critical first step in developing a thematic unit.

Barton and Smith (2000) also outline the important qualities of what they term "interdisciplinary outlines" (p. 55) but what I will call thematic units.

1. They should contain "meaningful content" (p. 55): material that is appropriate and "worth knowing"—not trivial—and includes logical connections between content areas.
2. The unit's activities should be authentic: ones chosen for "intrinsic meaning or application" (p. 56) and placed in meaningful contexts.
3. Students' needs should be a driving force behind these units: they are flexible and based on children's unique experiences, prior knowledge, and interests. I would add that students can be involved in actually planning units of study.
4. Because of this flexibility, thematic units particularly need "teacher mediation" (p. 61): the ability to match learning activities to children's needs and "to provide the scaffolding" (p. 62) to optimize learning.

5. Finally, thematic units require varied resources, including reading materials at different levels of difficulty, which are carefully evaluated for quality and usefulness.

Several scholars (see Norton, 1982; Pappas, Kiefer, & Levstik, 1999) describe one useful tool for organizing a thematic unit: a webbing process. This is a diagram of a mental process showing interconnections between related topics, learning activities, books, and other materials arranged around the central theme. This process is especially useful for showing how different concepts and content areas are integrated in natural ways. It also shows where there are gaps that can be investigated or considered. Thus thematic units are a vital means for literary learning about the intertextuality of literary works, their place in literature as a whole, and their relationship to all learning.

For good examples of thematic literary units there are a number of excellent sources. Nonfiction experts Evelyn Freeman and Diane Person (1998) emphasize the use of informational books in integrated units; see chapter 5 in their volume for webs of possibilities in content area learning. Joy Moss (1996), the inventor of "focus units," provides detailed examples of such units that are appropriate for grades 1 to 6. Language arts educator Gail Tompkins (1995) describes a "theme cycle" in action in a fifth-grade classroom focused on the American Revolution. These and other sources can stimulate our thinking about possible ideas for our own thematic studies with children.

MULTICULTURAL AND GLOBAL EDUCATION

We live in a society that is increasingly multicultural and global and in a world that is shrinking. These facts make education for such a diverse, mobile community and an international perspective imperative, and literature has an important role to play in this context. Rudine Sims Bishop's (1994) idea about children's literature as both a mirror and a window provides an illuminating metaphor for thinking about this role. All children need books in which they see themselves and their lives reflected, books that offer new insights about familiar themes. They also, however, need books that are openings into different lives in unfamiliar settings and are about less common (to the reader) ideas. These are vital for expanding readers' universe, for creating empathy and understanding about others.

In addition to exploring books that reflect diversity, children can learn to *read* multiculturally (Hade, 1997) or "against a text" (Nodelman, 1996,

p. 120). This means that it is not only up to authors to provide authentic representations of cultures in their writing; it also is the reader's responsibility to recognize and question the author's implicit assumptions. This is not just a matter of identifying inaccuracies that *are* included in the text, but also of seeing what is *not* there. Omissions are just as important as what is present. As an example of multicultural reading—and one probably intended to be so by the author herself—I explore Patricia McKissack's *Flossie and the Fox* (1986). First, though, in a straightforward reading, children can relate to the positive characterization of a young girl who outwits a sneaky fox—a classic literary triumph of the underdog. When a supposedly inexperienced and naive child encounters a creature that she doesn't recognize, she innocently introduces herself and inquires about the creature's identity. When he asserts that he is a fox, Flossie studies him carefully, proclaims that she doesn't believe him, and makes sly put-downs about his attempts to convince her of his authenticity. In the process, she skillfully diverts the fox's greedy attention from the eggs she is delivering to a neighbor. Children may delight in Flossie's spunkiness and cleverness and cathartically identify with her; they may cheer the child heroine's ability to overcome a creature often depicted in stories as the one from whom children and other smaller animals need to be rescued. These are supposedly universal themes of childhood with which all children can relate.

Still, Flossie also is identifiably African American, depicted not only through Rachel Isadora's illustrations but through Flossie's Black dialect as well. In contrast, the fox speaks in formal, pretentious English. He exasperatedly declares, "Of course I'm a fox. A little girl like you should be simply terrified of me. Whatever do they teach children these days?" To which Flossie saucily responds, "Well whatever you are, you sho' think a heap of yo'self" (unpaginated). Later, Flossie confides to a cat, "He sho' use a heap o' words." Finally, when the fox shouts in desperation, "This is absurd," Flossie tartly replies, "No call for you to use that kind of language." Flossie's cleverness, then, provides a subversive subtext in which an unschooled Black child overcomes an apparently well-educated character, perhaps meant to signify dominant White culture. More specifically, Black vernacular trumps standard English. This kind of multicultural reading could stimulate fruitful discussions among readers that raise issues about race and class. (Gender also figures, with Flossie as a girl and the fox as male.)

Another way of looking into mirrors and through windows is to recognize literary universality and uniqueness. One thing that literature provides is a better understanding of our own literary heritage and that of other cultures. By comparing and contrasting these heritages, we can see how they are similar and different. For example, readers can gain insights about how narrative patterns develop in various cultures. In Laurence Yep's *Dragonwings* (1975), the main narrative thread of Moon Shadow's adjustment to early 20th-century life with his father in San Francisco's Chinatown is interrupted by—or intertwined with—a long story about a Dragon King. This type of digression, which perhaps may be common in Chinese culture, is unusual in typical American plots for children.

Another dimension can be explored through folktale variants that appear in different cultures. The differences and similarities between Cinderella variants, to use a classic example, reveal interesting values and other qualities about the cultures they represent. (However, my very use of the label *Cinderella*, instead of *Yeh-shen* [Chinese and possibly the oldest version], *Maha* [Middle Eastern], or *Adelita* [Mexican], betrays my Eurocentric literary bias.) Poetic structures also present larger cultural traits. For example, haiku is a form that in itself typifies certain qualities of classic Japanese culture: their emphasis on nature, their understated simplicity, their celebration of details and moments that may often be overlooked, their subtlety and openness to individual interpretations, their ability to evoke rather than tell. Matthew Gollub's *Cool Melons—Turn to Frogs!* (1998) is an excellent introduction to haiku and the writing and life of one beloved Japanese poet and, thereby, a glimpse into that culture.

Finally, we can examine universality and uniqueness through themes. For example, a theme such as "making a living or achieving a dream often involves sacrifice and perseverance" offers abundant cross-cultural and international perspectives. In *Pedrito's Day* (Garay, 1997), a young Central American boy is saving money he earns by shining shoes to buy a bicycle. In Antonio Hernández Madrigal's *Erandi's Braids* (1999), illustrated by Tomie dePaola, a young Mexican girl helps her mother get enough money for a new fishing net (with which they make a living) and also a new doll by sacrificing her long, beautiful braids to the hair buyers. In Haiti, Ti Marie dreams of becoming an artist in *Painted Dreams* (Williams, 1998), but her family has no money to buy her paints, brushes, or canvas. Ti Marie perseveres by figuring out a way to attract money with her talent. Across the Atlantic in Nigeria, young Lateef in *Bicycles for Rent!* (Olaleye, 2001) also dreams of owning a bicycle, and Tololwa Mollel's *My Rows and Piles of Coins* (1999) portrays a similar situation for Saruni, a Tanzanian boy, who saves money he earns for a bicycle. In each of these books, child protagonists help their families make a living and at the same time achieve their own dreams.

The preceding examples demonstrate yet again how reading a set (or even pair) of books can enhance understandings about each of them. We notice qualities by comparing and contrasting a group of books that we might not see (at least, as easily) otherwise (Lehman & Crook, 1998), and we can gain new insights by examining one story in relation to others. This can be especially helpful when international books are linked with more familiar American texts. Recognizing the similarities between the more and less well-known contexts can help us to comprehend and appreciate the differences more fully. For instance, Eleanor Batezat Sisulu's *The Day Gogo Went to Vote* (1996), about a young girl who accompanies her great-grandmother to vote in the first multiracial election in South Africa in 1994, resonates with American readers who are familiar with similar events for African Americans, such as that portrayed in *Freedom's Gift: A Juneteenth Story* (1997), by Valerie Wesley, which commemorates the celebration of June 19, 1865, when slaves in Texas finally learned about their freedom. Readers who identify with Trisha's problems with learning to read in Patricia Polacco's *Thank You, Mr. Falker* (1998) will easily empathize with Sarie's dread of school because Sarie also struggles with reading in Niki Daly's *Once Upon a Time* (2003), set in rural South Africa. And older readers who grasp the bittersweet dilemma in Jean Craighead George's *Julie of the Wolves* (1972) faced by Julie/Miyax regarding the changing context for her indigenous culture in Alaska will recognize the same problems and choices confronting Be, a Namibian San (or Bushman) girl in Lesley Beake's *Song of Be* (1993).

The ultimate goal of multicultural and global education is to promote cross-cultural understanding, appreciation, and respect. Good literature creates empathy in readers, who, between the pages of books, enter the lives of others like and unlike themselves. As recognized by Jella Lepman (2002), founder of the International Board on Books for Young People, "the first messengers of . . . peace will be children's books" (p. 5), and their readers can help the world become a better place for all humankind.

MULTILINGUALISM

In furthering multicultural and global education and extending literary learning across the curriculum, multilingualism can be a valuable component. Languages represent the experiences and worldviews of the cultures that use them and, thus, are windows into diverse ways of knowing. Because of the capacity of multiple languages to extend children's thinking, I view language variation as an instructional asset, rather than a liability. These differences draw attention to language and create interest in the study of language. Jobe (1993) describes "language markers" as distinctive cultural patterns or ways of expression. We can use these to learn about cultures, as we encounter them in children's literature.

For example, South Africa recognizes 11 official languages, and although most children's books published there are written in either English or Afrikaans, many English-language books include liberal sprinklings of words in one or more of the other languages. These words may be identified and defined in a separate glossary in some books, but in others, readers are left to figure out foreign words from the context, which actually can be considerable fun as well as challenging. In *The Day Gogo Went to Vote* (Sisulu, 1996), colloquial expressions in Xhosa and Zulu (two dialects) are explained in a glossary, words such as "Gogo" (Grandmother) and "toyi-toyi" (a rhythmic movement often seen at celebrations and political rallies). However, other words in the text, such as "rand" (South African currency), require interpretation; and still other English words are used in unfamiliar ways (to American readers), such as "pensions office," "township," and "identity book." Dianne Case's *92 Queens Road* (1995) not only contains single Afrikaans words, such as "afdakkie" (a covered patio or veranda) and "stoep" (the step or porch of a house), but entire Afrikaans sentences spoken by characters, which in the American edition are translated into English. (Afrikaans is the mother tongue of not only many White South Africans, but of most "coloureds," as well.) All these examples add authentic flavor to the narratives and present opportunities for discussion and inquiry about language. They also can deepen readers' understanding of another country and the diverse cultures in it.

In the American context, Spanish is the most common second language, and there are a growing number of bilingual books being published that reflect this situation. Sometimes the two languages are presented in separate editions, such as Pat Mora's *Doña Flor* (2005), an original tall tale set in the southwestern United States. Other times, the text is presented in two languages in the same edition, such as *A Gift for Abuelita/Un regalo para Abuelita* by Nancy Luenn (1998), a story about the Mexican celebration of the Day of the Dead. In addition to language, each of these titles offers a wealth of information about the cultural and literary traditions of the Latino communities they represent.

Children's literary learning needn't be confined to a particular area of the curriculum, and using children's books across the curriculum is not just an interesting, even meaningful, way to introduce content. As teachers, we can structure a holistic program of literary study by recognizing its contribution to the entire curriculum. Our students will gain a deeper, more complex grounding in literature, and their literary development will be more well rounded. In the following chapter, we will examine how the classroom environment also influences literary learning.

6

The Classroom Environment and Literary Learning

WHEN I VISIT an elementary school class, I always take time to sit and look around the room. I notice how the room is arranged; what materials are available and how they are stored; how many and what kinds of books are available, where they are located, and how they are arranged; and what kinds of displays there are on walls, bulletin boards, shelves, and other surfaces. I often feel inspired by what I see and make note of good ideas I gain. As a former classroom teacher and now a teacher educator, I can always learn from other teachers' examples. One thing I know from my own teaching experiences and from observing others' is that just as literary learning can be nurtured by the whole curriculum, so can it be supported and enhanced by the total classroom environment, as captured in J. Patrick Lewis's poem "The Road Begins" (see epigram facing the contents page).

In this chapter, I discuss the physical arrangements of classrooms, classroom library centers and children's book collections, other literature-related materials, schedules and use of time, the social climate of the classroom, and parent involvement in supporting the total environment. With specific examples, I consider the relationship of these topics to literary learning.

PHYSICAL CLASSROOM ARRANGEMENT

The physical arrangement of a classroom reflects the teacher's philosophy about and approach toward literary learning. If we revisit the cycle of literary study proposed in Chapter 1, certain necessary qualities about classroom arrangement become clear.

In Phase 1

For reading and interacting with literature, students need the opportunity to read widely and reflect on their reading. This means that a classroom needs places where readers can be located comfortably, so they are able to do this. Beyond individual desks, elementary classrooms at all grade levels need inviting spaces demarcated by bookshelves, cubbies, rug areas, and moveable bulletin boards or chalkboards, for example, to create visual separations that are conducive to concentrated reading and reflection.

Such divisions have the added advantage of maximizing limited space in crowded classrooms, as I found when I taught in one particularly small room. Alternatively, children can learn how to create their own privacy in the midst of busy settings, perhaps with the aid of a cardboard trifold barrier they create, decorate, and set on their desks and a CD or tape player with headphones so they can listen to soothing background music while reading. A separate listening center for enjoying prerecorded books, on tapes or CDs, is an important support, especially for less independent readers. For my individual conferences with children about their reading, I placed two chairs with a desk or two chairs with desk arms together in a space between two bookcases, from which I could still observe the whole room.

In Phase 2

To share individual responses with others—whether in literary conversations or other response events, such as oral interpretation or dramatization—spaces where readers can gather in pairs, small-group literature circles, or as a whole class are required. Small groups can meet at tables, desk clusters, or some other space where they can sit in a circle on the floor or on chairs. Tables or desk clusters enable readers to face each other while hearing and sharing comments and insights, while rows of desks hinder such interactions. Places to create literature-inspired displays, such as an art center (located near a sink and water supply), and cupboards or shelves where materials for making them can be stored should be included. For displaying such artwork or other visual projects, shelves, extra tables, bulletin boards, and even windowsills are needed. I also provided a space where a small group could meet to develop and practice dramatizations and puppet shows in response to reading. Finally, for large-group sharing of response events, as well as listening to literature read aloud by the teacher or a student, a communal rug area with a focal point toward a comfortable seat (I used a rocking chair) and an easel (on which to display a flannel board for storytelling, chart paper for writing, or posters and other charts) provides a good setting.

In Phase 3

Promoting literary growth can and will happen in any of the above settings: that is, in one-on-one conferences, teacher-led small groups, or occasionally with the whole class. In addition to the spaces I've already described, I found it necessary to sometimes give whole-class instruction in a more formal setting with students seated at work tables or desk clusters and a chalkboard or dry-erase board and overhead projector for ready use. More sophisticated technology, such as a smart board or computer with projector, are also valuable assets for large-group instruction. Teacher-led small groups need a table around which to meet. This might be either one of the regular student work tables or a separate special, often kidney-shaped table. Finally, learning centers where individuals, pairs, or small groups can explore literature across content areas make an important contribution to holistic literary growth.

Overall, the physical arrangement needs to be flexible. As activity requirements change, spaces need to be rearranged and furniture moved, especially if the classroom itself is fairly small. Less space will mean that any given area must be used for various purposes, and furniture that is easily moved and has multiple uses is more adaptable and serviceable. Figure 6.1 shows one diagram of my fourth-grade classroom.

CLASSROOM LIBRARY CENTER

The centerpiece of a literary classroom is the library center, with its literature collection. I wanted this to be the most easily recognized and inviting area in my classroom—one that everyone entering my room noticed immediately and one to which my students were strongly drawn. Even though there should be a school library, a classroom collection is essential for promoting children's interest in reading and the amount of reading they do, according to research cited by Lesley Mandel Morrow (1982). Furthermore, as noted by classroom teachers Jann Fractor and Marjorie Woodruff and teacher educators Miriam Martinez and William Teale (1993), availability of books alone is not sufficient; the design of the classroom library also is important. Unfortunately, in their study of kindergarten through fifth-grade classrooms, very few (only about 11% of the 81 classrooms that did contain library centers) met their criteria for good or excellent classroom libraries, while about

Figure 6.1. Classroom Layout

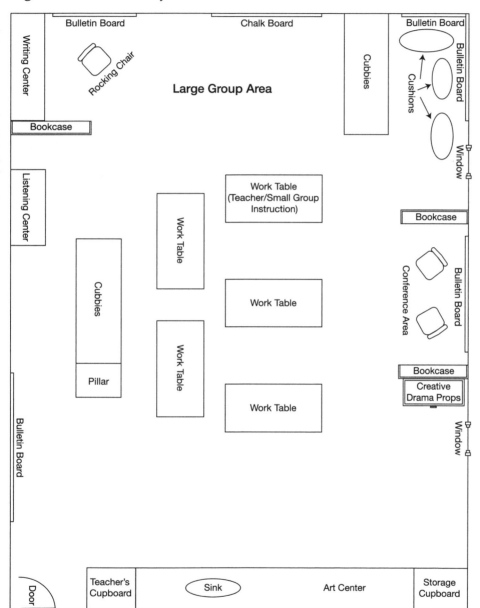

89% were merely "basic." What are the elements of excellent classroom libraries? According to these researchers, such library centers are partitioned from the rest of the room; have carpet or seating; are quiet and well lit; contain some open-faced display of books; have a name; include other literature-related props, such as a flannel board, book jackets, or posters; and can hold at least five children. Some teachers in classrooms I've observed use a decorating motif, such as pirates as in *Edward and the Pirates* (McPhail, 1997), that relates to the name of the library center, for example, Digging for Treasure in Books.

Starting with the physical arrangement in my classroom, I partitioned the library center with bookshelves on two or three sides and furnished it with a rug and large cushions. (Other teachers I know have even included easy chairs or couches. All these, including cushions and rugs, can be picked up at thrift stores for little expense.) Some bookshelves were the standard variety, on which books were placed spine facing outward; other racks were open faced, to display the books' full front covers. In the latter instance, these might be special books on a particular theme, topic, or genre being studied. There were books organized by difficulty level or other categories developed by children, such as books in a favorite series, in separate bins.

Encouraging children to think of ways to categorize books is a valuable source of literary learning in itself. This activity helps students notice connections between books—an attribute of intertextuality—and gradually to develop some of the same literary categories, such as genres and books by special authors or illustrators, which adults use. Categorization also is a way to highlight some of the literary features that may be discussed in Phase 3, such as themes, characters, or settings. Finally, teachers can learn much about their students' understandings and interests by observing how they categorize books.

According to Fractor and colleagues (1993), excellent classroom libraries contain a minimum of eight books per child, which can be a rather daunting standard, especially for new teachers. However, with creative thinking and a little effort, it does not take long to reach this goal. For one thing, most school or public libraries will allow teachers to check out a large number of books for up to a month. If a teacher indicates what topics the class is studying, librarians will even collect the books in advance and have them ready for checkout. I quickly built my own collection of children's books for the classroom library by visiting secondhand bookstores and thrift shops, public library book sales, and yard sales. I joined a children's book club, making the orders available to my students for purchase and using the accumulated points to obtain books for the classroom. Finally, I encouraged my students to place any books they owned and wanted to share with their classmates in our library center for the year or as long as they wished. (Many left their books with me permanently.)

I know other teachers who have secured classroom library books through parent support projects (such as book fairs), grants, and corporate donations or by negotiating with their school districts to allocate a portion of the reading materials budget for trade books instead of more worksheets or other commercial reading materials. Publishers, or favorite authors through their publishers, can be contacted about donating surplus books or perhaps in connection with an author visit to the school. Finally, a school could create a book cooperative in which teachers share their books when titles are not in use and borrow others to use for a defined time period.

In selecting books for the classroom library center, I had several factors in mind: my students' interests and reading levels; their cultural backgrounds and experiences; my own knowledge of literature appropriate for the age levels I was teaching; literary quality (book reviews and award winners provided guidance in this area); authentic presentation of diversity; relevance to topics that we studied; and variety of genres, authors, and illustrators. It is important to include folklore, poetry, biography, and informational books. Within fiction, children need a varied diet of contemporary and historical realism, fantasy, and science fiction. Favorite authors and illustrators should be well represented, but so should those who are less familiar and with whom readers should become acquainted. Often I would introduce a new author to my students through a read-aloud selection and make other books by that writer available for students to read on their own. (Further considerations about the teacher's role in book selection are addressed in Chapter 7.)

Finally, remember to include picture books, even in classrooms with older students. For one thing, some highly sophisticated picture books, such as David Macauley's *Black and White* (1991) or David Wiesner's *The Three Pigs* (2001), may be more fully understood by older readers. For another thing, some older children who are, for example, delayed readers or English-language learners, will need the support of easier picture books in order to succeed as readers. For these students, practicing to read a picture book aloud to younger readers gives them the justification to read such a book and the opportunity to read the book multiple times, which increases their fluency and expression. Finally, sometimes literary growth, even with older readers, can be promoted best by using picture books that are excellent short stories in their own right, as suggested by Coughlin and Desilets (1980) in connection with Leo Lionni's *Frederick* (1967). Children are never too old to enjoy illustrated books if they are permitted and encouraged to do so. (I also included children's magazines and newspapers, among them *Cricket, Stone Soup,* and *Highlights for Children* in the library center.)

In my classroom, we developed a simple but effective borrowing system. I secured a large number of library book pockets from the school librarian, and as books were added to our collection, the classroom librarian (one of the student weekly helpers) attached a pocket inside the books and created a card with the title and author's name to insert in the pocket. A child who wished to sign out a book wrote his or her name and the date on the card and placed it in a file box. There was no time limit for keeping the books, but if another child wanted a particular book that was checked out, the borrower was required to return the book when it had been out for at least 2 weeks. (This sign-out system could all be done on a computer, of course.)

OTHER LITERATURE-RELATED MATERIALS AND EQUIPMENT

In research I have conducted with colleagues (Lehman, Freeman, & Allen, 1994; Scharer, Freeman, Lehman, & Allen, 1993), the importance of materials to support and enhance children's interactions with books became apparent. Interviews and visits with classroom teachers in kindergarten through grade 7 (a total of 19 across both studies), who indicated strong interest in using literature, demonstrated that these teachers gave careful thought to materials needed for book-related projects, such as bulletin boards and other displays of children's responsive artwork. One teacher created topical book backpacks that contained books, related objects, suggested activities, and a journal in which to record responses. Children took these "bookpacks" home to read and complete with their parents. Over time, this teacher had developed enough packs for each child in her class to have one at any given time.

In my own classroom library center and beyond, I displayed both publishers' book posters and book jackets (all laminated for durability) and ones created by children as response activities. When children created other book-related projects, such as dioramas, murals, collages, and mobiles, these also were displayed, often spilling out into the hallway, thereby extending the literary invitation to other classes and generating further enthusiasm for reading. These art projects can be made with many recycled supplies, including egg cartons, wallpaper-sample books, fabric scraps, and paper towel tubes, along with other supplies found in craft stores, such as yarn, raffia, and buttons. At the beginning of each school year, I sent home a list of supplies (most of which, as noted, are recycled and, therefore, free) that we needed and encouraged parents to send in anything they could. Whenever our stock ran low, I resent the list.

In addition to making displays, children "published" their own books, which were added to the classroom library as further reading material. Supplies such as paper and drawing instruments for the pages and cardboard and cloth for the binding were available for making these books. In classrooms where big books are used, children can help to create these enlarged versions of favorite patterned language picture books. They will have more ownership of these books, and these young helpers will enable a busy teacher to make more of these books for classroom instruction and individual reading pleasure.

Computers are an important asset in literature classrooms for producing text and designing illustrations and other graphics for student-authored books, for using the Internet for research or finding and corresponding with authors and illustrators. Children also can use computer applications to do response activities for books they have read.

For story retellings, children will use flannel boards with pictures they have drawn or roller theaters through which they can scroll scenes to retell stories or books they have read. For puppet reenactments of stories, children can create their own puppets from materials that are available in the classroom, write their own scripts, and perform a show with a puppet stage constructed out of a discarded refrigerator box or simple wooden frame. A box of versatile props, such as stuffed animals, police officer's badge, or medical worker's jacket, can assist with creative dramatic presentations related to books. The listening center needs a cassette or CD recorder/player with headsets. CDs or cassette tapes of children's books, plus copies of the actual books themselves for reading along, should be regularly updated and changed. Children can develop their own recordings of favorite books, thereby practicing their oral reading in a meaningful way and contributing to the supply of recorded books available for others to hear.

All these materials need to be stored appropriately on shelves or in cupboards, drawers, or bins. These places should be labeled clearly so that children can reach the items they need without having to interrupt the teacher's work with another child or group. I taught my students to return materials neatly when they finished using them and to notify me in writing when any supplies were running low. I emphasized that our classroom community could only function well if we all worked together to keep it organized.

SCHEDULES AND USE OF TIME

In a literary classroom, children need time for extended engagements with literature: reading and interacting with books, sharing responses with other readers, and developing as learners about literature (the three phases of the literary cycle). Rigid, highly segmented schedules are not conducive for these kinds of undertakings. Thus teachers are wise to maintain as much flexibility as possible and to organize time in the largest blocks permitted within their schedule constraints. For primary teachers this typically is not too difficult, but upper elementary grade teachers may find this challenging.

Workshops

Teachers at all levels have found that the "workshop" concept (Atwell, 1987; Calkins, 2001) provides a useful metaphor and structure for organizing instruction for reading and writing. Workshops incorporate the ideas of sustained periods of engagement with meaningful reading and writing experiences in which "apprentices" (students) learn from master "artists" (teachers) and other more proficient peers (Robb, 2000). In a literary classroom, the workshop can encompass both reading and writing together. Literacy researchers Ray Reutzel and Robert Cooter (1991) have proposed a model schedule for workshops as follows: a whole-group opening period of 15–25 minutes that includes sharing, a minilesson by the teacher, and discussion about what students will be doing for the next portion of the workshop; a block of 35–45 minutes in which students engage in independent reading, meet in literature circles, or have individual conferences with the teacher; and a final wrap-up time of 5–10 minutes for sharing what students accomplished. This workshop of about 70 minutes total time can easily be expanded from 90 minutes to 2 hours, if the schedule permits. I would modify the middle segment to follow different procedures for the teacher on alternate days: 2–3 days a week holding individual conferences with children and 2–3 days a week meeting with small groups for teacher-led instruction or with literature circles. Ideally, I also would want more than 5–10 minutes for closure and cleanup. (See Figure 6.2 for a sample schedule.)

In departmentalized settings, such as many upper elementary classrooms, the workshop concept can be modified. I taught fourth grade in a semi-departmentalized structure with 40-minute periods and 5-minute breaks in between. Within these constraints, it is very helpful if some periods can be doubled up, effectively creating 85-minute blocks of time, as I was able to do. Thus, I held individual conferences (while other students worked individually or in self-directed small groups) three periods a week, had a double period of small-group and individual work followed by oral presentations or book discussion groups on alternate weeks, a period of writing or editing workshops with various-sized groups, and one period a week for some type

Figure 6.2. Sample Schedule

½ hour	Whole class (present a lesson, explain assignment, answer questions)
1 hour	Conferences or small groups/ (Alternate) Individual work time
½ hour	Cleanup and closure

of whole-class lesson. Three days were double periods, making it possible for scheduled activities to expand or change as needed. (See Figure 6.3 for my schedule.)

Minilessons

Minilessons (described by Atwell, 1987, and Calkins, 2001) are relatively brief (often as short as 5–10 minutes, but sometimes extended to 20 minutes) whole-group instructional sessions in which the teacher presents and

Figure 6.3. Schedule for Fourth Grade

Monday	*Tuesday*	*Wednesday*	*Thursday*	*Friday*
		PERIOD 1		
Conferences/ individual work time	Small groups/ individual work time	Small groups/ library	Whole class	Writing, editing workshop
		PERIOD 2		
	Oral presentations Book discussions (Alternate)	Conferences/ individual work time		Conferences/ individual work time

demonstrates a specific strategy or concept. Reutzel and Cooter (1991) suggest that topics for these lessons derive from students' "observed needs," "teacher-selected skills" from district curriculum mandates, and "literature preparation . . . activities" (p. 550). Reading teacher and staff development expert Laura Robb (2000) describes three types of minilessons: *planned*, *impromptu* (in response to teachable moments that arise), and *review*. Thus, minilessons can be on any relevant topic, and they are highly useful for Phase 3 of the literary cycle, promoting literary growth. They offer teachers the opportunity to guide students' growth as literary learners in developmentally appropriate ways to make their interactions with literature more meaningful and pleasurable.

Individual Conferences

Finally, individual conferences are an important strategy for learning about and supporting students' individual development as readers of literature. (They also, however, can provide teachers with information on which to structure small-group instruction when similar needs are found among children.) Specifically, in my classroom, conferences provided the opportunity for students to share what they were reading independently with me and for me to learn about how well they could orally read a selection and what meanings they had constructed so far about the books they shared with me.

As noted by Marcia Popp (1996), these conferences require advance preparation by both the teacher and student. In my case, I would select three students each conference day to meet with me for about 15 minutes apiece, scheduled on a biweekly, rotating basis. I would review my notes from the previous conferences with them, plus any observations I had made about their work in the intervening time, and tentatively plan what I wanted to check, teach, and assign for the next conference. Students knew approximately when their next conference would be scheduled and were required to meet that deadline with any assigned work from the previous conference. They had to rehearse a self-selected passage from a book they were reading currently and bring that with them to read aloud to me. They also brought any written work they were assigned at the preceding conference and any questions they wanted to discuss with me about their reading, such as new vocabulary, puzzling ideas, or unfamiliar information. Once a conference started, it was uninterrupted time with me. I stressed the importance of this rule with the whole class and the need to respect every student's right to have my undivided attention for these few minutes. Students valued this special time and usually treated others as they wished to be treated.

To begin the conference, I would ask the child to read to me the rehearsed passage, while I made notes about the quality, such as fluency and expression, of his or her oral reading. When that was finished, I might respond to something I noticed in the passage and then would usually just ask the reader to tell me more about the book: what he or she liked about it, why it was selected, what connections had been made to personal or other reading experiences, and what questions he or she had about the book. Some teachers like to ask more structured questions, and sometimes I would ask follow-up questions related to ideas the student shared. However, I was careful to ask the kinds of questions described in Chapter 3 that were open ended and invited higher-level thinking. I might also suggest another related book that the child would enjoy reading next. Finally, I would collect and briefly discuss any completed written work that had been assigned at the previous conference and make new assignments for the next conference. If I noticed any individual needs with oral reading, the student would be instructed how, for example, to practice reading more expressively. I might have the child record any unfamiliar vocabulary in a personal dictionary and develop definitions based on the contexts in which the words were used. If the child was struggling with plot progression, he or she might develop a diagram or comic strip to depict it visually. If the child was having trouble picking a book to read or difficulty selecting one at an appropriate level of difficulty, I gave hints about how to make choices. Then we would conclude the conference, I would take a short break to answer other students' questions, and the next conference would begin.

Many times I would see needs in these conferences that I had noticed with other students also. In that case, I would not make individual assignments with each child separately but would plan to bring a group together for a specific lesson. Thus, individualized instruction (teaching to individual needs and interests) did not necessarily mean one-on-one instruction and became both more efficient and offered opportunities for learning through social interaction. These groups were organized on the basis of a particular need and for a single lesson or two, such as those described in Chapter 3.

THE SOCIAL CLIMATE

One of the most inspiring examples found in children's literature, for me, of positive social climate in a classroom is *My Great-Aunt Arizona* (Houston, 1992). In her tribute to her very special relative, Gloria Houston describes Arizona as a child of the Blue Ridge Mountains who "loved to read—and dream about the faraway places she would visit one day" (unpaginated). When she grew up, she became a teacher in the same school she had attended, and she passed on her passion for reading about faraway places to her students. She also "hugged her students" for 57 years; "She hugged them when their work was good, and she hugged them when it was not" (unpaginated). This truly seems the embodiment of an ideal social climate for literary learning.

According to Roe, Smith, and Burns (2005), a positive social-emotional environment includes "establishing a community of learners, creating a learning-centered classroom, and providing motivation" (p. 504). By hugging her students whether their work was what she expected or not, Arizona created a safe community in which her students would be more likely to take risks and support each other. By teaching them about distant places, she encouraged them to learn and think about life beyond their small hometown, and when she shared her love of reading, she gave her students the motivation to *want* to read in addition to the *ability* to read. I believe that this desire is the most significant test of a true reader.

Lucy Calkins (2001) writes about the use of minilessons as more than strategy instruction; they are also "an opportunity to shape the values of our classroom community" (p. 67). What are some of these values in a literary classroom? Drawing upon the core values of this book, I suggest the following:

- First, and uppermost, is love for literature and the ability to immerse oneself in a literary engagement.
- Second is freedom for individual choices about what to read, when, where, and with whom.
- Third is sharing and valuing different readers' perspectives and constructing new insights as a community.
- Fourth is challenging each other's points of view respectfully but honestly.
- Fifth is regard for the discipline and training of the mind to become readers who find increasing pleasure in reading that is personally meaningful and rewarding.

PARENT INVOLVEMENT

Any teacher understands the importance of parent involvement in children's learning; the role of parents in supporting a positive classroom environment for literary learning is vital. I've already mentioned several ways that parents can contribute, but there are additional ones that teachers can encourage.

First and most important, parents can read aloud or listen to their children read books that are brought home from the classroom, school, or public libraries. As noted by Wells (1986) in his 15-year longitudinal study of all the literacy-related activities that occurred in homes, children listening to stories read aloud had the greatest correlation with school achievement. Even parents or other adults in the home who cannot read to children can listen to the young ones read, or, as the grandma did in Eve Bunting's *Wednesday Surprise* (1989), learn to read *with* a child, using the same books the child is reading.

Another important contribution that parents (even those who can't read) can make is to tell stories to their children. This is an important way to build children's sense of story from birth and also to pass on family stories and cultural heritage, such as demonstrated in Sandra Belton's depiction of an African American community's "telling place" in the evening in *From Miss Ida's Porch* (Belton, 1993). If students, in turn, bring these stories to school, they can be written and made into books for the classroom library—as noted earlier, a way of both adding to the number of books and enriching the cultural climate in the class.

Teachers can reach out to parents by encouraging them to take their children to the public library—perhaps even accompanying the class on a field trip to the library or inviting the public librarian to speak to parents about the library at an evening school meeting. For parents, such as undocumented immigrants, who don't feel comfortable providing the information needed for a library card or who don't have time for such visits, teachers can help by creating literature bags of classroom books sent home with children (see earlier discussion about bookpacks) and a list of meaningful literature-related activities that families can enjoy together. Teachers also can encourage parents to allow their children, when they are old enough, to stop by the public library on their own after school as a place to read quietly and find books with the help of a friendly librarian.

As a classroom teacher, I compiled lists of suggested titles that I thought my students would enjoy and sent these home to parents before vacations and holidays as gift ideas. I encouraged parents to consider buying books in place of toys that easily break and have a limited life span. If I wanted to give my students a special reward for something, I presented them with a quality paperback book (obtained through book club points) instead of another prize.

Parents can be invited to school to give talks and to volunteer to read or work with individual children. This is an excellent way for busy teachers to maximize the help and attention that students need for optimum learning.

It also involves parents directly in the literary life of the classroom community and can bring students into contact with a wider variety of adult role models.

Finally, we need to respect family priorities with time as we offer these suggestions, encouraging parents to participate to the extent they can and thanking them by establishing an inclusive spirit geared toward parents' supporting the literary environment. In the following chapter, I will address specifically the teacher's role in this environment.

7

The Teacher's Role

IN BARBARA COONEY'S *Miss Rumphius* (1982), young Alice sets out to accomplish the three things in life she learned from her grandfather: visit faraway places, find her place by the sea, and do something to make the world more beautiful. For the third—and most difficult—task, she sows bushels of seeds around her village by the sea from which lovely lupines bloom and spread year after year, adding joy to the lives of all who live there. Like Miss Rumphius, what I tried to offer my fourth graders and what I still hope to give my university students and classroom teachers is something to make the world more beautiful—the wonder and power of literature—and I tell them to pass the gift on to others. And like Miss Rumphius's three accomplishments or like traditional story patterns that often have three parts or episodes, in this chapter I offer three considerations about the teacher's role in that endeavor: where the locus of control resides, how to make decisions, and being a "curator" of literature (Eeds & Peterson, 1991).

THE LOCUS OF CONTROL

By now it should be obvious that the teacher has a crucial role to play in creating a literary program for children. However, there are distinct contrasts between a classroom that is highly teacher directed and one that is largely student centered. Teachers need to find an appropriate balance along that spectrum that works best for literary learning in their settings, and in that search for equilibrium, I describe six issues that guide my thinking.

Implicit Versus Explicit Instruction

First, I need to consider the appropriate uses of implicit and explicit instruction. Sometimes all that teachers, like Miss Rumphius, need to do is scatter the right seeds and beautiful things will happen on their own. Young readers can learn many important and essential concepts about literature just by being in a highly literate environment. Certainly, love for literature and fundamental pleasure in reading can be conveyed naturally by a teacher's attitude and example. In addition, the classroom environment (see Chapter 6), the kinds of books that we choose and how we read them aloud to our students, and the encouragement and time for interacting with literature and sharing responses (including our own) with other readers all make implicit contributions to literary learning. As one dynamic first-grade teacher recently told me about her classroom— which was covered, floor to ceiling, with literature-related and other kinds of written texts, such as charts and posters, etc., and with artifacts—even if her students were just staring at the walls during class, they were learning something.

Effective teachers also know, however, that there is a time and place for explicit literary instruction. This is most beneficial at the point of need or when students show us by their comments and insights that they are ready to learn a new concept. When we seize those opportunities, we have the chance to offer "just right" lessons that help children become more capable, insightful, and educated readers. (This is sometimes referred to as the "Goldilocks principle": instruction that is neither too hard nor too easy, but just right. It also correlates with Vygotsky's "zone of proximal development.") As teachers, we need to be alert and ready to take advantage of those "teachable moments" and times when students are ready for the next step. To help in catching these clues from students, we need ways to document them for making instructional plans, an issue I address later in this chapter.

Building on What Children Know

Second, one of the ways that we can provide appropriate explicit instruction is by listening closely during literature discussions and scaffolding onto the ideas that students raise. I can help prepare myself to do this by planning in advance ideas that I hope to raise, and if I hear something from students that relates to the ideas, I can interject the appropriate idea—often by asking a question, or shooting the "literary arrow" (Eeds & Peterson, 1994)—for them to consider in the context of the conversation. Other times, I just need to be ready to help a discussion build in its own direction—which may be unexpected—by asking probing questions or offering my own ideas related to the topics.

The Teacher's Effect on Readers' Stance

A third issue that I consider is my influence on children's stance as readers. One notable aspect of stance has been identified by Rosenblatt (1980, 1991) as the continuum between aesthetic and efferent reading, a theory I discussed in Chapter 2. She cogently explains that teachers play an important role in determining the kind of stance (efferent or aesthetic) that young readers will take toward any particular text, and, therefore, we as teachers must be clear about our purposes for reading. She further asserts that an aesthetic stance is the most appropriate initial transaction with a literary work, and Joyce Many's (1990) investigation of eighth graders' literary responses showed that responses "written from the aesthetic stance were associated with significantly higher levels of understanding" (p. 61). Many (1991) later confirmed this finding with fourth and sixth graders also. Another way of viewing stance through children's responses to literature has been classified by researchers as text based or reader based (Lehman & Scharer, 1995–1996; Wollman-Bonilla & Werchadlo, 1999). This classification refers to the focus of readers' attention as they respond to literature, whether more from their own personal feelings, reactions, and experiential associations with the text or from their understanding of and insights about the text itself (see Chapter 2).

Many and Wiseman (1992) went on to examine the influence of teaching approach on third graders' reading stance as exhibited in the children's free responses to literature after hearing a picture book read aloud. Responses of the classes that engaged in follow-up discussion were closely aligned with the nature of the discussion, whether based on the literary *experience* or on literary *analysis*. Likewise, Pantaleo (1995) found that the prompts teachers gave for fourth- and fifth-grade students' journal responses to literature and the feedback they provided about those responses "influenced both the students' beliefs about the characteristics of a 'good' response and the content of the children's responses" (p. 44).

Studies such as these, I believe, support the importance of what I have been advocating in literary discussions: Begin with children's initial, personal responses; listen closely to what they say; be ready to ask questions that link to the ideas they raise and that will encourage them to consider their ideas more deeply or in new ways. Sometimes, as Wollman-Bonilla and Werchadlo (1999) found with first graders, the best questions or responses from teachers are simply "What do you think?" (in response to children's questions, soliciting their thoughts before providing my own ideas), "Why do you think so?" (asking children to give reasons to support their thinking), or "Tell me more" (prompting children to develop their ideas more fully) (p. 605). I believe that I can use my influence on children's stance as readers to encourage them to read aesthetically, draw on their personal experiences, and build on these to nurture their literary development and ability to reflect more analytically about why the text causes them to respond as they do.

The Teacher's Influence on Literature Discussions

This relates directly to my fourth consideration: my influence as a teacher on classroom literature discussions. Research in which I participated (Scharer, Lehman, & Peters, 2001) illuminated the nature of discussions about *Amos & Boris* (Steig, 1971) and *Whales* (Simon, 1989)—examples of fiction and nonfiction texts, respectively—in fourth- and fifth-grade classrooms. We found that discussion topics about these two books focused most heavily on their literary (personal response, evaluation, plot, themes, and language) and informational (characteristics and activities of whales, endangerment of whales, comparisons of mice and whales, and unfamiliar vocabulary) aspects.

Even more relevant to the present discussion was what we found regarding *how* the discussions evolved. First, teachers dominated the discussions by asking nearly all the substantive questions. Furthermore, most questions that teachers asked were factual level (information recall and virtually always efferent) rather than higher level (interpretive, open ended, and more likely to be aesthetic). Finally, teachers dominated the discussions by initiating most of the topics and by using a talk pattern of teacher-student-teacher, rather than student-student. Relevant implications are that the types of questions we ask influence children's stance toward reading and that teacher dominance signifies a classroom with a strong locus of control with the teacher. If I want literary discussions to be more child centered and responsive to young readers' developing insights, then I need to think carefully about the type, level, and number of questions I insert in guiding the conversations and find ways to actively encourage more student than teacher talk.

Providing Choices for Children

My fifth issue concerns providing choices for students. Simply stated, the more I offer children options about what to read and when, where, and with whom, the more student centered my classroom will be. In addition, the more choices students have about how they will respond to texts, the more opportunities this should give them to respond aesthetically (Cox & Many, 1992). At the same time, I am not suggesting that these choices need to be unlimited. Teacher guidance (and even a certain level of control) has a beneficial role in children's literary development. Thus, a reasonable number and type of options (which can vary according to the circumstances) from which children may make selections often is appropriate. In providing these choices, I tried to offer ideas that employed varied response modes, such as art, writing, creative drama, and oral interpretation, as discussed in Chapter 3.

Book Selection and Censorship

Finally, I must consider book selection for my classroom. I work in an area of the United States where children's books have been challenged in local schools, and, as a classroom teacher in other locations, I faced this issue. Most teachers will be confronted with it at some time, so it is a real concern. As a teacher, I tried to select books carefully for classroom use that I considered essential to the learning situation and that I could defend as such. I articulated my literary and educational reasons and even found it helpful to write them for any books that seemed potentially controversial. If a parent objected to a particular title, I would offer an alternative choice for that parent's child, but I would not allow one parent or a small group to dictate what the rest of the students could read.

Two further points should be stressed. The first is community standards. Educators need to be sensitive to what most parents in the particular school context believe is appropriate for their children (Galda & Cullinan, 2006). Parents and the school board should be consulted about what these standards are and, in turn, should learn about literary standards and why certain books that may be controversial are educationally important. Teachers and school librarians can play an important role in educating about and advocating for children's literature. Cultivating a positive relationship over the issue of book selection often enlists parental support for teacher decision making.

Second, it is very helpful if the school has developed a written policy and set of procedures for handling complaints. If such guidelines do not exist, teachers should work with administrators to get them in place. Professional organizations such as the American Library Association, the National Council of Teachers of English, and the International Reading Association provide useful information and even suggested forms on their Web sites for dealing with censorship attempts. Teachers who are prepared for such experiences will be better able to find the right balance between freedom and responsibility. Book selection is one kind of decision teachers face; planning other instructional choices is what I address next.

MAKING DECISIONS ABOUT INSTRUCTION

As teachers, we make instructional decisions constantly: before, during, and after the actual lessons and learning experiences. This is one of the most crucial aspects of a teacher's role and distinguishes teachers as professionals from teachers as technicians. Professional teachers retain our right to decide about the teaching and learning in our classrooms. We know our students and the classroom and community context best, much better than do outside forces such as administrators, curriculum developers, textbook publishers, legislators, and other advocacy groups. We are able to gather appropriate data to make sound decisions, and we can use a variety of best practices to implement those decisions. We do not need a how-to manual to tell us what decisions to make or what procedures to follow, although we do seek good practical ideas from many sources (including whatever teachers' manuals may be provided). At the same time, professional teachers have the obligation to stay current with theory, research, and innovative practice; to know appropriate resources, including literature; to understand our students; and to be aware of and responsible for district, state, and national mandates. We also bear responsibility for articulating our vision and decisions about literary learning to stakeholders such as parents and administrators.

The Students

Teacher educator Patricia Crook (1995) discusses many variables affecting teacher decision making in literary classrooms, but I focus here on two: the students I am teaching and the curriculum that I am responsible for covering. First, if I am going to offer "just right" lessons, I need to know my students well, and, in addition to all the typical ways we become acquainted with others, teachers need to plan and use some intentional means for gathering information from children. These techniques are often called "kid-watching" (Goodman, 1986; Pappas, Kiefer, & Levstik, 1999), and they involve teachers' watching and listening to students.

To help me record and organize what I see and hear about children's literary development, I have identified many useful strategies that generally fall into one or more of three broad categories. Yetta Goodman (1989) classifies these as observation, interaction, and analysis. *Observation* is watching and listening, *interaction* is talking with children about what I have observed, and *analysis* is determining what those observations and interactions, plus the products that students create, mean. Key to all these modes of kid-watching (or authentic assessment) is their continuous nature; "assessment . . . often feels like an ongoing conversation. One exchange is unlikely to contain all the information I need about a student" (Fenner, 1995, p. 241). A holistic picture of a student's development emerges from gathering varied data over an extended period of time. Kid-watching also focuses on what children are *trying to do* and *can do*, rather than on what they do *not do*

(Hancock, 2004) and should be interpreted from the perspective of literary developmental patterns, as discussed in Chapter 2.

For literary assessment, I will want to learn about the reading tastes and response preferences of my students (Hancock, 2004), their amount and level of engagement with literature, and their growing understanding and interpretation of literature. Fenner (1995) describes the kinds of "vital signs" (p. 242) that we can monitor in children's learning: how students select books to read and how successful they are in their choices; when and why children abandon books they start reading; the quality of their "interpretation and reflection" (p. 245) about what they read; what children discuss about books in casual, unplanned conversations; what kinds of "world building" (p. 247) or envisionments (Langer, 1995) children exhibit as they engage with literature; how students' reading affects their writing; and what connections they make between literary works and with their lives and other learning experiences.

To get more specific about these "vital signs," I offer several examples of ways I used to glean information about my students' literary growth.

- First, to learn about their *amount of reading*, I kept a log of all the books my children read. I did this in the form of a "book bank"; students made a "deposit" to their "book accounts" whenever they finished reading a book. They and I could review their book accounts to see how many books they had accumulated. I also would observe how much time children chose to spend reading; anecdotal records are a good means for keeping track of these observations.
- Second, I obtained clues about their *reading tastes* by examining the titles of books in students' book accounts for patterns of preferred genres, favorite authors, topical interests, and how much they challenged themselves with more difficult material.
- Third, I learned about children's *response preferences* by keeping track of the types of activities they chose in demonstrating their response to and understanding of books they read. For example, I noted on a checklist whether an activity was a piece of writing, a creative dramatic presentation, a visual art product, or something else. A quick scan of the checklist told me *what* students did; I used rubrics or written comments to assess the *quality* of these activities.
- Fourth, I could discover children's *level of engagement* (and "world building") with their reading through the quality of ideas and insights they expressed in literature discussions, in individual conferences with me, and in their response journals and what they displayed in their response activities.

- Fifth, these same means showed me students' *growing understanding* about literature and literary concepts. I could analyze written products with rubrics or checklists, discussions with checklists or anecdotal notes, and conferences with notes written on a cumulative log for each child. Folders or portfolios, I found, were a good way to organize written and some artistic products.
- Sixth, students revealed their *literary interpretations*, again, through response activities of all types. In addition, I observed their oral interpretation of literature (through their use of expression to convey meaning) in individual conferences, when students read aloud to me, and in their ability to convey characterization, for example, in creative drama productions. These types of oral demonstrations can be captured and analyzed later with video recording.
- Finally, I watched for *literary connections* that students made in their writing (particularly response journals), in literature discussions, and in casual conversations with other children or me. This last I tried to remember and preserve in anecdotal records.

These examples are not exhaustive, but the main point is that everything children do provides clues to the quality and extent of their literary learning. Alert teachers try to capture samples of as many different kinds of evidence in varied settings and across time as possible. Figuring out what works best as we gather, organize, and analyze this data is part of every teacher's professional responsibility. For further specific examples, Hancock (2004) offers excellent concrete tools, such as checklists and rubrics, to use in documenting young readers' literary learning.

The Curriculum

The other major variable in decision making that I want to discuss is the curriculum. There are control issues here as well. Every teacher is both responsible for and somewhat constrained by national, state, and local mandates, which have an enormous impact on curriculum, or what teachers are supposed to teach. Curriculum is important, Crook (1995) notes, as "a coherent framework that will guide teachers . . . so that experiences for children in later grades build on those that occur in the earlier school years" (p. 74). However, if educators are not vigilant, outside forces, such as mandates and assessment requirements, can drive the curriculum, instead of what we know is best for children's developmental needs and the local context.

As a classroom teacher, I used the official curriculum as one important source of information, but since I couldn't teach everything in the curriculum at the same time, I would start with the areas that best matched my students' needs and interests (derived from my kid-watching). When we finished with those requirements, and as the children developed further, we would move on to new concepts that best met their growing levels of understanding. The point is, I made the decisions about what parts of the curriculum to teach at any given time based on my knowledge of my students' current development. This meant that I did not follow a prescribed sequence, nor did I teach exactly the same things in the same order from year to year. The good news is that most of the nine teachers whom we interviewed in our study of teachers' beliefs and practices (Scharer et al., 1993) also retained their right (and responsibility) to make curricular decisions, suggesting a level of confidence (at least at that time) among teachers committed to literature that is important for instructional autonomy.

With this freedom, however, comes responsibility for setting appropriate learning goals and accepting accountability for student learning. Information about children's literary development needs to be used, not merely gathered. I can only use this information if I organize it systematically, analyze it carefully and regularly, and understand what it means. Based on my best insights, I set tentative learning goals for all my students and plan instruction to meet those goals. As I teach, I continue to "monitor the vital signs" of my students to determine if the goals are achieved. If they aren't met, I adjust either the goals or the instruction and try again until I get it right, because ultimately I hold myself accountable for my children's literary learning.

In the real world, teachers also know that we are held accountable by outside forces, even as we assert our authority as decision makers. Thus, I offer some thoughts about dealing with these constraints. First of all, I have stated throughout this book that literary teaching need not detract from time spent on teaching skills or content. In fact, teachers can do both at the same time by thinking about the links between skills, content, and literary learning in a different way. I have detailed the means for finding such linkages throughout this book. Therefore, in a literary classroom such as I have described, students should be able to learn the skills and content needed for success in standardized tests.

Having said that, some teachers have learned to cope with testing pressures by explicitly teaching their students how to take standardized tests. If we think of these assessments as a genre of writing, like other genres, children need to learn *how* to read them in order to make sense of them. The strategies for taking tests, just like any other learning strategies, can be taught and practiced—and need not consume much time. Short, focused minilessons, accompanied by clear reasons for why the class needs them, should be the most effective and encroach the least on time needed for learning other things.

BEING A "CURATOR" OF LITERATURE

What I have addressed about understanding children's literary development relates to my third consideration about a teacher's role: his or her knowledge base. Eeds and Peterson (1991) liken the teacher's role in literary instruction to that of an art museum curator. To be a curator, one needs to be highly knowledgeable about not only the particular works in that museum but also their relationship to the larger world of art. Being a curator also connotes both devotion to building and maintaining the collection and passion about sharing it with others. Roser (2001) states that "as curator . . . the teacher uses the particular lexicon of literature study—the language informed readers use" (p. 215); I would add that a good curator teaches that language to others (students) so that they can become more proficient and find increasing pleasure in their experiences with literature (addressed in Chapter 1).

Sloan (2003) describes the teacher's knowledge base as a "deductive framework" about "the unifying principles of literature" (pp. 152–153). With this structure in mind, "the teacher devises learning sequences that allow students to inductively discover" those principles (p. 153). This means that I don't typically use direct instruction to impart information to children, but with a strong literary foundation myself, I can use that knowledge to create developmentally appropriate literary experiences through which my students can make their own discoveries about literature. In turn, I, as a knowledgeable curator, can provide further learning opportunities that build on the children's emerging insights.

How does a teacher build a knowledge base? Nodelman and Reimer (2003) offer several ideas, of which I find three to be most helpful. Most of all, we need to be avid readers of literature ourselves. This is the single best way to widen our knowledge of literature as a whole. Second, we can deepen our understanding of literature by reading published literary criticism, from which we can gain other knowledgeable readers' (the critics') insights about the texts we are reading and consider them in relationship to our own perceptions. Third, we can read articles in professional periodicals, for instance, *Journal of Children's Literature, Children's Literature in Education, Language Arts*, and *The Reading Teacher*, and professional books to learn about innovative methods for literary teaching and literary terminology, such as explained in the Glossary in this book (Appendix A). We may find novel ideas in these sources that work well with our students.

To these suggestions, I would add three others. Many readers gain additional pleasure and literary understanding from joining book clubs, and teachers are no exception (Vardell & Jacobson, 1997). Such interaction with other readers gives us the added benefit of multiple perspectives. In addition, I continue to grow as a teacher of literature by attending professional conferences and workshops, where again I gain new ideas and have the opportunity to interact with other teachers who share my concerns and priorities. When I meet and listen to authors, illustrators, and literary scholars at these conferences, I learn about and often reach new insights about their work that I can use with my students. Finally, besides these self-directed ways to build my knowledge, I grew immensely by taking graduate courses in children's and young adult literature. This is one of the best ways to stay current in the field and to find mentors and peers who are committed to the same goals for literary teaching and learning with children.

In this chapter I have cataloged the varieties of "seeds" I study as I strive to emulate the role of Miss Rumphius. In the following, and last, chapter, I address how to get started and move forward in creating appropriate programs of literary study with children.

8

Getting Started, Moving Ahead

S IXTH-GRADE TEACHER Donna Peters (1995) recounts her journey
from being a traditional teacher of *reading* to becoming a literary teacher
of *readers*. For her, it began with a basic "change of attitude and beliefs,"
which she says "was the easy part. The hard part was knowing where to start"
(p. 35). For me, change started with frustrations I faced during my early un-
pleasant experiences with teaching reading in a traditional fashion. Then
graduate study of children's literature in a master's program sparked my
decision to completely revise my approach and to make literary study the focus
of my literacy program. Like Peters, I spent several years refining that approach.
Now, in this final chapter, I describe the steps that I have found useful in the
process of initiating an appropriate literature program for children.

DEVELOPING AND ARTICULATING A PHILOSOPHY
OF LITERARY STUDY

The first step is forming a coherent philosophy of literary study, well grounded
in sound research and theory. This brings me back to the discussion that began
in Chapter 1 regarding the need for theory, which serves as an important
road map in this journey. Without theory, teachers are traveling ahead without knowing where they are going or how to get there. Theories about literature and the reading of it and theories about children and their learning
(such as those described in Appendix B) all help to inform teachers of what
their destination should be and how they are headed there. From these various theories, teachers must form their own philosophy, or overarching set
of directions, and they must be able to articulate this philosophy clearly to
themselves and others. At the same time, a philosophy is not written in stone
but evolves and changes with new experiences, information, and insights,
while remaining consistent with one's core values and principles.

SETTING GOALS

The next step for me was setting goals for myself as a teacher that matched my philosophy. When I reentered the classroom after getting a master's degree, I composed a list of goals that I developed from what I learned in my graduate program. I wrote these goals in a notebook, adding more goals as the first year progressed. Periodically, but particularly at the end of each school year thereafter, I assessed my progress in attaining the goals, checking off the ones I had accomplished. At the beginning of each new year, I reexamined my philosophy to see if it matched my current understandings and experience. Then I recomposed my list of goals, keeping those for which I still needed to strive and adding others for that year.

I'll admit that I am a list person, so this method worked to keep me motivated; other strategies may work better for other teachers. However, there are two points I will make about goals: (1) it is important to have goals toward which to aim in order to be the best teacher one can be, and (2) when a teacher reaches goals, new ones should always be set. In other words, while celebrating what has been attained, a teacher should not allow him- or herself to become complacent and remain at that point in the journey. Teachers need to challenge themselves constantly to go further. For me, this is the secret to staying fresh and excited about teaching. I did this process on my own, but occasionally a whole school staff develops a common set of goals, such as one elementary school that developed a 5-year plan to move from basal readers to literary texts (Scharer, 1992), which can provide tremendous support for individual teachers.

STARTING SMALL, BUILDING GRADUALLY

Like children, teachers develop over time, and as in our approach to children, we should give ourselves permission not to attempt everything at once and to make mistakes along the way. In looking at my goals for the year, I realized that I couldn't accomplish them all at the same time, so I started with ones that I thought I could most easily attain. I needed to keep the long view in mind, but I also needed to recognize that I would get there one small step at a time and to celebrate each milestone that I passed.

For example, in the first year I implemented some choices for book response activities and in subsequent years developed more options. I selected some books for literature circles the first year and added more selections later.

I refined individual conferencing strategies from one year to the next. I added to my repertoire of book talks each year. I learned new ways to infuse skills instruction or content areas with literary learning. I learned how to be a better kid-watcher and how to use that information to plan more effective learning experiences.

Completing each goal gave me satisfaction and the confidence to strive for more, and so on. In this way, I gradually over the years built a program of literary study that came closer and closer to my ideal. Ultimately, like the engine in Watty Piper's classic *The Little Engine That Could* (1978/1930), I realized that I *could* succeed if I kept chugging along and believing that I would make it.

Part of the trip, though, involved experimentation and trying out ideas until I got it right for my students, my teaching context, and myself as a teacher. Sometimes I made mistakes or had to reverse for a short time, but I tried not to let that throw me off course; rather, I learned and made corrections.

DEALING WITH CONCERNS AND FRUSTRATIONS

The process I've described was never as smooth as it perhaps sounds. Along the way, I was confronted with many obstacles that were daunting and discouraging at times. Some of my concerns paralleled those of teachers whom Scharer (1995) surveyed, who were making the transition from a basal program to reading literature, as I discuss here. One of the most important issues was the amount of time it took me to plan and prepare for literary teaching. Since I wasn't following a prepackaged program, I had to invent nearly everything. I had to make the literature selections and plan how to use them with my children, including questions, activities, and materials to accompany the texts. Since I wasn't doing the same lessons with the whole class, I had to organize not only what students were doing with me, but also what they were doing on their own. I typically worked longer hours than many of my colleagues, but it was worth it when I witnessed my children's literary development and love for literature. In addition, each year of teaching was easier because I didn't have to create everything new from one year to the next but could build on what I had planned and prepared before.

A second issue I faced was obtaining materials, such as trade books, and using materials that were mandated by my school. I've already described in Chapter 6 how I built my classroom library collection. I've also suggested a number of ways that I adapted the basal materials I was required to use, such as choosing the story selections that had the most literary value and potential for my children's interest, implementing any suggested activities that were meaningful and creative, and generally developing my own questions to stimulate students' higher-level, critical thinking.

A third issue, which also affected planning time, was evaluation. Like Scharer's (1992) teachers, I found that knowing how to assess children's literary development was not immediately obvious. First, I needed to determine *what* learning to evaluate, since I didn't have a literature curriculum to follow, and then I had to decide *how* to authentically evaluate that learning, since I didn't use traditional tests as learning indicators. Instead, I had to create alternative evaluation measures, such as the kid-watching techniques I've described in Chapter 7.

A fourth concern related to lack of support, which can range from indifference to outright disagreement with other teachers and administrators, unless you are in a situation such as the one Scharer (1992) describes, with the whole school making a transition together. I found myself in a number of different contexts over the years, but Sorensen's (1995b) advice to find a support group can be very useful. Look for another teacher or teachers who can be mentors for you, or offer to mentor new teachers who can benefit from your experience. Working with novice teachers can be very inspirational. Try to find a corps of teachers in the same school or district who share a teaching philosophy and goals similar to yours and who are willing to meet as a study group or share ideas by Listserv. Conferences, workshops, and professional organizations (such as the Children's Literature Assembly of the National Council of Teachers of English, the United States Board on Books for Young People, the Children's Literature Association, and the Children's Literature and Reading Special Interest Group of the International Reading Association) are also good sources of compatible, enthusiastic colleagues. Check their Web sites for contact information.

MAKING THESE IDEAS WORK FOR YOU

Concerns and frustrations such as those described above can, with creative problem solving, become opportunities to make the ideas I've outlined in this book work for you. Start with the ones that sound most interesting and possible, try them out, make adaptations as needed to fit your situation, invent new strategies that meet your needs and context—whatever it takes to create the best possible program of literary study for your students. There is nothing sacred about what I've suggested; you have the power to make your own decisions. Always remember, though, to take the long view, as Frew

(1990) did retrospectively about his 14-year evolution from a basal-bound teacher to one who is "comfortable" as a literary teacher. Know where you are headed, and be true to that vision. Like the eagle in Christopher Gregorowski's retelling of an African tale, *Fly, Eagle, Fly!* (2000), we are meant to soar, in our case with literature, and not be grounded, as the eagle is with the farmyard chickens. Take your children with you, and celebrate their flight.

Appendix A:
Glossary of Literary Terms

THE LITERARY TERMS used in this book are included here with brief explanations. For more in-depth discussion of many of these terms, readers may consult a particularly helpful resource, *The Concise Dictionary of Literary Terms* (Baldick, 2004).

Alliteration: The repetition of (usually initial) consonant sounds in close succession. Most often used in poetry, it is also employed in prose to achieve a particular desired effect of sound.

Allusion: A (sometimes oblique or indirect) reference to another literary text and its characters, plot, etc. Allusions usually are not explained but instead rely on a reader's familiarity with literature to make sense.

Archetype: An element—such as a character, theme, or setting—that recurs so often in mythical or traditional literature that it comes to symbolize a recognized pattern. *Good versus evil* is an example of an archetypal theme; a hero or heroine in search of a quest would be another archetype. Although archetypes may be thought of as universal concepts, they are actually culturally bound.

Characterization: The manner in which a character is developed and portrayed. Characterization can be revealed through direct description; the character's speech, actions, or thoughts; what other characters say, do, or think regarding that character; and what the author or narrator conveys.

Foreshadowing: A literary device that provides a hint, clue, or warning that something will occur. Foreshadowing provides suspense but also enables the alert reader to make predictions about what will happen.

Genre: A category or type of literary writing. Genres can be as broad as fiction and nonfiction or more narrowly defined as folklore, fantasy, realistic fiction, poetry, biography, informational books, and picture books. Within genres there can be subgenres, such as high, low, and science fiction within fantasy. According to Moon (1999), different genres require different reading practices.

High fantasy: A subgenre of fantasy, set in an alternate world or a mythical, imaginary land within the present world. High fantasy often involves a struggle between good and evil and a hero or heroine who embarks on a quest or exhibits other archetypal traits. Many high fantasies come in a series, such as Lloyd Alexander's *Prydain Chronicles*, C. S. Lewis's *Chronicles of Narnia*, or Philip Pullman's *His Dark Materials* trilogy.

Imagery: Often regarded as what readers see in their minds while reading a text, but also can be induced through other senses, such as taste or smell. Images can become symbolic if they evoke significant patterns, as in the way that the rolling prairie in *Sarah, Plain and Tall* (MacLachlan, 1985) reminds Sarah of the rolling sea she misses near her home in Maine.

Intertextuality: The awareness of interconnections between literary texts (one level of intertextuality). These links may be such things as similar themes, characters, or narrative patterns. Archetypes are grounded in intertextuality; allusions or references in one text to another create intertextuality. The interrelationships also can involve another level of texts, such as films, songs, and various other cultural artifacts. Generally, the more one has read and experienced, the more intertextual connections that a person can make.

Irony: An incongruity between what seems to be or what is stated and what actually is. Sarcasm is a blatant form of irony; however, irony often is a much more subtle, but intentional, inconsistency.

Literary canon: A set of literary works that are regarded as particularly important or essential by whatever authority is establishing it. Such authorities often are literary scholars, who typically are members of a dominant group; thus, a literary canon may come under attack or criticism as being culturally biased by individuals who feel more marginalized. For example, scholar E. D. Hirsch, well-known proponent of "cultural literacy," has published numerous lists of "essential knowledge," in works such as *Books to Build On: A Grade-by-Grade Resource Guide for Parents and Teachers* (Hirsch & Holdren, 1996), constituting a canon that has been criticized as Eurocentric.

Literary conventions: Practices that are accepted or prescribed by custom or general agreement. Fairy tale beginnings ("Once upon a time") and endings ("And they lived happily ever after") are examples of conventions. Happy endings in children's literature are another convention.

Literary device: Any recognized literary technique, such as foreshadowing, symbolism, irony, or imagery.

Literary elements: The devices that compose fiction: character, plot, theme, setting, style, and point of view.

Magic realism: A style in modern fiction that includes some element or situation that is fantastic, surreal, or highly improbable in an otherwise seemingly realistic narrative. *Holes*, by Louis Sachar (1998), is an example of magic realism in children's literature.

Metaphor: A figure of speech that is an implied comparison between two things. For example, calling the *fleeing* of people from persecution a *flight* is a comparison of their action to that of birds literally flying. When Templeton, a real rat in *Charlotte's Web* (White, 1952), behaves like a rat (being greedy, selfish, and devious), his species becomes a metaphor for his behavior.

Mood: The feeling that a reader gets from a text or illustration. In writing, it is conveyed by the author's tone as developed by choice of words, while in illustration, it is created through the artist's choice of color and media.

Motif: A recurring element or pattern in literary texts—similar to an archetype, although usually not as significant. A magic pot or other magical object, being granted three wishes, being put under a spell, magical beings (such as a witch), and tricksters are examples of common motifs from folklore.

Narrative: A story, or a set of events arranged in a particular order, constituting a plot. Fiction is narrative literature, as is some poetry that tells a story; some nonfiction, such as biography and even other forms that convey information in a story format, are also narrative literature.

Narrator: The voice that tells (or that the reader assumes is telling) the story. Narrators can be one of the characters in a story or someone who stands outside the story but can see and know all, such as the author or implied author (see **point of view**, below). Furthermore, narrators can be reliable (someone a reader can trust) or unreliable (someone whose account may be misleading or self-serving).

New Criticism: A type of literary criticism that focuses on analyzing the meaning of texts through close reading of the works in and of themselves, without regard to the reader's characteristics or the historical, social, political, and cultural contexts in which the texts were created or are read.

Pace: The speed at which a narrative seems to the reader to move. Plots that are action filled usually appear to move at a faster pace, while plots that are more introspective may seem to move at a slower pace. A plot may seem to drag, especially for young readers, when not much is happening in the story.

Plot: The selective arrangement of events in a narrative, from an introduction of the characters, setting, and a problem or conflict to the actions taken to overcome or solve the conflict to the resolution of the problem and an outcome. The sequence of events may or may not be chronological.

Point of view: The perspective from which a story is narrated. The story may be told in either a first-person voice (the "I" voice) or in a third-person voice (also known as "limited omniscient") by one of the characters, or it may be told by an omniscient, all-knowing voice. Some narratives are told from multiple points of view.

Protagonist: The main character in a story. Usually readers identify most closely with the protagonist.

Quest: A journey undertaken by a hero or heroine in a search for some symbolically important object (such as the Holy Grail in the King Arthur legends) or for someone (as in Meg's search for her father in *A Wrinkle in Time*, L'Engle, 1962).

Setting: The time and place in which a story occurs. A setting can be explicitly identified or vague (such as a contemporary story in an unnamed urban area). It can be integral to the story and even highly symbolic (such as Narnia) or merely serve as the backdrop to the story (as in *Sylvester and the Magic Pebble*, Steig, 1969). Fairy tale settings often are conventional, as expressed in "once upon a time in a kingdom far away."

Structure: The manner in which all the elements of a literary work are organized into a coherent whole. It also includes how those elements relate to each other and form patterns.

Style: The way that a text is written, including, among other elements, language, humor, tone, symbolism, irony, sarcasm, creation of suspense, and imagery.

Suspense: A feeling of anticipation or apprehension about what will happen next in a story. Suspense can be heightened by cliff-hanger chapter endings and can be both created and alleviated by foreshadowing.

Symbol: Something that signifies or represents something else. Often a concrete object or person represents a larger significant idea. For example, when Max returns home in *Where the Wild Things Are* (Sendak, 1963) to find not only his supper waiting for him but also that it was still hot, that event can symbolize his mother's love in spite of his wild behavior.

Theme: A significant, deeper meaning that reveals the author's purpose. Themes should emerge indirectly (except in fables where the theme or moral is stated explicitly) and are constructed differently by various readers. Themes can be made didactic if teachers talk about them as "lessons."

Tone: The overall atmosphere of a work, such as serious, humorous, or depressive. Tone is similar to mood. It expresses the author's manner or attitude to the reader, which can be honest, respectful, or condescending, for example.

Appendix B:
Literary and Child Development Theories

I DEFINE *literary study* for this book as teaching and learning that begins with children's present responses, understandings, interests, and experiences with literature. There is no preset curriculum, but as children reveal their current literary knowledge in classroom discussions and activities regarding books, teachers will look for ways to build upon those existing concepts. Using language, examples, and explanations that children can grasp, alert and supportive teachers will help children grow beyond their present state of literary development to ever-new levels.

Literary Theories

More than 20 years ago, Brett and Huck (1982) identified three major categories of literary theory: "work-centered criticism, child-centered criticism, and issues-centered criticism" (p. 879). According to them, *work-centered criticism* focuses primarily on the text itself and analysis of it; *child-centered criticism* looks at the relationship between a child reader and the text; and *issue-centered criticism* examines the presentation of societal topics in texts for children. These categories are fairly broad and simplistic, but they were very helpful to my thinking as a graduate student, and I have found that they do account, in one way or another, for most literary theories. My intention here is to provide an overview of the major theories that are most relevant to children's literature—one that is comprehensible (but not necessarily *comprehensive*) and, I hope, practical for teachers. I also want to acknowledge that different scholars may define and name theories in various ways.

Reader Response Theory

As May (1995) notes, many elementary teachers are at least familiar with reader response theory, so that is where I begin. According to this theory, most often associated with Louise Rosenblatt (1938/1995) and by extension with Wolfgang Iser (1978), literature is the experience between a reader and a text, and the reader has a primary role in constructing the meaning of the text. In fact, according to Rosenblatt, the literary work does not exist until it is literally created in the transaction between reader and text. In this view, literature is created anew each time a different reader interacts with a text or even when the same reader interacts with a text at different times. Therefore, this theory would fit within the "child-centered" category identified above; Beach (1993) classifies it as an "experiential" theory.

One of the criticisms about this theory is that since there are potentially millions of readings of any text, every one of those readings can be considered a literary work, making it hard to privilege any one reading over others. Indeed, teachers sometimes think this means that literary interpretation is completely subjective and none is better than another. In practice, then, they might simply elicit and accept students' responses without any deeper thinking or critical examination of those responses. However, Rosenblatt did not intend for her theory to be applied in this manner. She asserts (1974) that "the literature program should be directed toward enabling the student to perform more and more fully and more and more adequately in response to texts" (p. 353). Presumably, this means that teachers (and other readers) have a role to play in "enabling" and evaluating what are "adequate" responses.

Psychological   Theories

These theories, also, since they are located within the reader, belong to "child-centered" criticism. They include child development and psychoanalytic theories applied to literary interactions, always beginning with the inner state of the child reader. Coupled with Rosenblatt's theory, the work of Jean Piaget has influenced our understanding of reader response since the 1970s: that cognitive developmental stages of thinking affect readers' responses to literature. Thus, children think qualitatively differently about a given text from how an adult might, and even children at different cognitive levels (who may or may not be the same chronological age) think differently from each other. Also implicit is the notion that adults can identify (based upon knowledge of child development theory) characteristics of books and individual titles that are appropriate for different developmental levels. In other words, if we understand the way children think at different stages, what kinds of books will likely match their needs and interests? Leading theorists, such as Arthur Applebee (1978), J. A. Appleyard (1990), and Nicholas Tucker (1972), have described children's literary development from this perspective in considerable depth.

Psychoanalytic theories also focus on the reader's inner self and are based on Sigmund Freud's work on the unconscious. The child psychologist Bruno Bettelheim applied Freud's theory to children's literature, particularly fairy tales in which children's subconscious wishes and dreams or nightmares are released in safe ways. For example, a young child who is punished by her mother can displace her anger indirectly by imagining her mother's demise as a wicked stepmother. Whereas it would not be acceptable to wish that her real mother would die, hearing that fantasy come true about a witch or stepmother in a fairy tale, such as "Hansel and Gretel," is a psychologically safe resolution for the child. Bettelheim goes on to explicate in graphic detail the underlying Freudian meanings of several well-known fairy tales in his book *The Uses of Enchantment* (1976).

Critics of developmental and psychoanalytic theories raise several objections. First, developmental theory—while recognizing that developmental levels are not sharply delineated stages and that not all children at the same age will be at the same cognitive level—views children who are at the same cognitive level as more alike than different, without recognizing their many, important individual differences. Thus, to say that children of a particular developmental level likely will respond to a given text in a certain way does not account for the actual range of responses of real readers.

Another problem raised about developmental and psychoanalytic theories is that, by placing such strong emphasis on the inner self, they don't acknowledge the importance of social and cultural contexts on readers' responses. Factors such as ethnicity, gender, or prior experiences with literature all influence how individual readers respond to the texts they encounter. Finally and relatedly, the theories in this category all were developed by White, Western males; it is highly probable that their views and ideas were shaped by their own experiences and may be quite different from the perspectives of many readers who don't share their backgrounds. These concerns noted, however, psychological theories can usefully inform our thinking about how the development of individual children can affect their literary needs, interests, and responses.

Social and Cultural Theories

Brett and Huck's (1982) category of issue-centered criticism is too narrow to encompass the range of social and cultural theories, but these theories do often relate to societal issues. Lev Vygotsky's sociocultural theory of child development has been applied to literary theory (by Stanley Fish, 1980, and others) to demonstrate the importance of the social (classroom or other) context in which literature is read and discussed. Because meaning is constructed in an interpretive community, different readers' perspectives on a common text have a profound effect on their experience of the literary work. In addition, their perspectives are influenced by the teacher and his or her stance toward literature (e.g., Many & Wiseman, 1992) and by students' roles in the classroom, such as "leader, facilitator, devil's advocate, outsider . . . class clown, teacher-pleaser, burnout" (Beach, 1993, pp. 108–109).

Readers also operate within particular cultural contexts related to ethnicity, age, sex, religion, language, or class, and cultural theories seek to identify the influences that these and similar factors (the "isms") have on response to literature. Feminist, Marxist, or multicultural critics (such as Harris, 1994, and Trites, 1997), for example, view literature and the acts of reading and interpretation as cultural artifacts shaped by the ideologies of authors and readers and the contexts in which reading occurs (for example, an urban classroom in which the teacher is female, White, and middle class or an after-school book club in a community center). Cultural theories help readers to uncover the values of a work (which often reside as much in what is *absent* from the text as what is *in* it) by "reading against the text" (Nodelman & Reimer, 2003, p. 156). At the same time, the closer the book's ideology is to the reader's values, the more difficult it becomes to recognize or uncover that ideology because it may be taken for granted and assumed to be true.

According to Beach (1993), social theories are limited because they don't take into account the broader cultural context outside the classroom, while cultural theories can be simplistic (in the same way that developmental theories are) by treating readers as members of groups, rather than recognizing their individual differences. (Similarly, criticism of the men who created the psychological theories discussed earlier casts them as potentially biased because of their presumed membership in a particular group.) Further, as Beach states, "a major limitation of cultural theories [is] their deterministic stance" (p. 152) in that readers will respond to literature in particular ways because of their group memberships. However, social and cultural theories both work positively to broaden our understanding and interpretation of literary works and to lessen the privileging of one particular, "correct" reading. They also have influenced markedly work-centered criticism, which we consider next.

Textual Theories

Traditional text-based (that is, work-centered) theory, known as New Criticism, which was favored in the 1930s, or formalism, focused on texts and their analysis by highly educated critics, who believed that ideal interpretations could be developed and transmitted to less-knowledgeable readers. The teacher's role was to convey these meanings to students, and individual, unique responses were devalued. (According to May, 1995, this perspective is the basis of much current reading instruction.) Reaction to New Criticism, led in part by reader response theorists, caused textual theorists to take a new approach—one that built on reader response to return to the text to examine it for what *in the text* caused that response. In order to do so, therefore, readers must understand literary conventions and structures and have the language to describe and discuss what they see in the text. (This is where the teacher's role, as envisioned by Rosenblatt, comes in, and it is in this sense that Beach, 1993, includes textual theories in his book on reader response theories.) Thus, published criticism and teachers' interpretations are not the only correct readings. They are simply other readings that can be helpful (or not) to less-experienced readers.

However, a potential flaw in these theories is their implication that the work is a constant, while Rosenblatt's (1978) idea is that the literary work (or "poem") is an "event" or experience. Practically, this means that different readers will construct and attend to different aspects of the text, making it at least somewhat fluid. And as I have discussed above, *what* readers construct is influenced by their development, unconscious desires, the cultural contexts from which they come, and the social interactions that take place in a community of readers.

Archetypal Theory

Mythic or archetypal theory, as developed by Northrop Frye (1957), also is a type of work-centered criticism. It views all literature as interrelated and growing out of the ancient patterns of mythology, which can be classified into four categories: romance, tragedy, irony-satire, and comedy (Sloan, 2003). Furthermore, according to Frye, literature can be arranged hierarchically through a series of four "displacements" or modes from pure myth through romance and mimetic (realism) to ironic. As Wolf (1985, quoted in Nodelman & Reimer, 2003) suggests, each mode requires "an increasingly sophisticated reader" (p. 231), and the progression "provides a logical way of organizing the literary experience of children from least displaced to most displaced" (p. 231).

Although, indeed, much of the earliest literature to which children are introduced is in the realm of myth, legend, and folklore (arguably the roots of literature), Frye's (1957) heavy reliance on European, Christian archetypes may (though not necessarily) limit the application of his theory to literature from other cultural traditions. In addition, there is always the problem of placing individual stories into discrete categories. Frequently, they overlap or contain elements from more than one category, and questions can be raised about the value of applying such a scientific approach to literature. However, by trying to locate stories that we read within Frye's categories, over time literary patterns emerge that can help us to see the place of individual texts within literature as a whole and to build gradually a coherent structure that gives the reader "a sense of literature as a continuous journal of the human imagination" (Sloan, 2003, p. 35).

Each of these literary theories has value for shaping our understanding of literature, and each has some limitations, as I have described. They have evolved over the years as thinking has changed from viewing the text (and the author who wrote it) as the primary "authority" to a view of the nature and centrality of the psychological transaction that occurs between a reader and text as the "literary experience" to a recognition of the influence of the social and cultural context in which literary experiences occur. In my view, the theories work well collectively if we view literary transactions as flowing in multiple directions. In other words, texts influence readers' response, and readers create the literary work. Social and cultural contexts shape readers' responses, and readers influence social and cultural variables. Texts are authored in particular social and cultural milieus and, in turn, affect the social and cultural environment not only of that day but also through subsequent generations, if they last. Likewise, child development theories, which are presented next, evolve over time as our understanding of children has changed and continues to grow.

Child Development Theories

My intention here is not to provide an exhaustive overview of all child development theories, but to touch on those aspects that I believe are most salient to the study of children's literature. First, though, a definition: *Developmentally appropriate practice*, or instruction, refers to a specific approach to teaching children based upon widely acknowledged principles of child development (Berk, 2003). Teachers plan and implement instruction by careful observation of children and understanding what types of practices are appropriate for children's optimal development. Typically, instruction is more appropriate for younger children when it emphasizes hands-on, individualized, and small-group methods; firsthand experiences that are relevant to children's lives; and use of concrete materials. Older children, however, can employ more abstract, symbolic approaches, particularly if they are related directly to ideas and experiences with which they already are familiar. Again, the curriculum, rather than being determined outside the actual classroom context, evolves from individual children's real needs, abilities, and experiences. Children are taught at the right time and in a manner fit for their personal and collective growth. Thus, the literary study that I envision is developmentally appropriate instruction. Now, for the relevant theories.

Psychosocial Theory

Erik Erikson refined Freud's psychosexual stages of development to show how children confront and resolve key personality development conflicts, which are embedded within specific cultural contexts. The stages most relevant to teachers are initiative versus guilt (whether children will be allowed to experiment and take initiative or will be too strongly controlled by adults), industry versus inferiority (whether children will feel competent), and identity versus identity confusion (whether adolescents will gain a sense of self and purpose in life).

The implication that this theory has for literature concerns what themes will best meet children's psychosocial needs in each stage. Books that address these themes and show characters facing these issues likely will be ones that children can relate to their own lives and concerns. In addition, the idea of initiative suggests the importance of allowing children to make their own choices about what to read. Adults can offer or recommend titles that we think might be appropriate, but the selection is up to the child.

Social Learning Theory

The importance of modeling for shaping learning is the central tenet of Albert Bandura's theory. More recently, he has recognized the role that cognition plays, as well. If children learn by observing (and thinking about what they see), it's not hard to imagine how literature can influence children's behavior and sense of self-efficacy. Literary characters with whom children can identify engage readers in imagining solutions to problems and give them a sense of vicarious accomplishment through those resolutions. Children then can apply or adapt these models to their own lives.

Growth Motivation

Abraham Maslow's hierarchy of needs explains how human development is motivated by the satisfaction of lower-level needs before higher-level needs can be attended to. Once the two lowest need levels (physiological and safety) are met, literature can help to satisfy the needs for belonging and love (in stories containing these themes), esteem (the respect readers can gain from sharing their insights about literature with others), and self-actualization (realizing one's potential as a result of having one's imagination and intellect stimulated). Further, literature obviously plays a large part in meeting cognitive (learning and knowledge) and aesthetic needs, in addition to the hierarchy of basic needs. Encouragement for wide reading and conversations about books are important ways that teachers can help children to meet their needs for optimum growth.

Cognitive Developmental Theory

Jean Piaget's comprehensive theory not only describes the stages of children's cognitive development but also accounts for *how* children learn. The three stages most relevant to teachers are preoperational (in which children begin to use language and symbols in their thinking), concrete operational (in which children can think more logically but are still tied to concrete, hands-on experience), and formal operational (in which older children and adolescents can think abstractly). The way that children develop from one stage to the next is by constructing their own knowledge. (Thus this theory often is known as "constructivist theory.") Adults can provide experiences that promote children's discoveries and ask questions that make them think about their findings. As children encounter new concepts, they adapt (through assimilation or accommodation) those ideas to fit their mental schemas. When they meet situations that challenge their existing knowledge, children feel disequilibrium that spurs them to adapt their understanding. Adults play an important role in both generating such experiences and in helping children to resolve their cognitive dissonance.

The implications for teachers and children's literature are, first, for teachers to know where their students are on the developmental stage continuum and to provide books that match those stages. For example, knowing that children in middle elementary grades, ages 8–10, typically are developing a stable concept of time and that they understand past and future, are becoming more flexible in understanding right and wrong, are "questioning death" (Huck et al., 2004), enjoy fantasy, and increasingly need to feel competent might suggest that a book such as *Tuck Everlasting* (Babbitt, 1975) would be a text that many children in this age range would enjoy. Its themes of the positives and negatives of living forever; making choices for life; ethical and moral decision making that is not always clear cut; and good, old-fashioned adventure could appeal to these children's cognitive, emotional, moral, and literary understanding and promote their further development.

Second, in order to grow, children also need books that challenge their current understandings and push their comfort levels. Supportive teachers offer those books as well and are there to help children through the discomfort. For example, although many children (even into middle school) tend to prefer books with happy, tidy endings, teachers with sensitivity and good discussion skills can introduce their students to books such as *Bridge to Terabithia* (Paterson, 1977) in the upper elementary grades and help them work vicariously through the issue of losing a close friend or loved one.

Finally, the idea that children construct their own knowledge complements Rosenblatt's theory of the reader creating the literary work. Literature and literary understanding cannot simply be transmitted to children; they experience and create those for themselves. No matter how important we believe our insights are about a book we are discussing with children, we cannot demand that they accept those ideas for themselves. Rather, we can offer our thoughts as fellow (and even more experienced) readers along with those of other readers, as discussed in the next section.

Sociocultural or Social Constructivist Theory

Lev Vygotsky added new insights to Piagetian theory by demonstrating the importance of language and social interaction in children's development. Children grow best in settings where they work (and talk) with others to create shared understandings, or intersubjectivity. Optimum learning happens in the individual child's zone of proximal development, the mental place in which the child is capable of learning with more expert guidance, but within his or her present cognitive potential. Adults play an important role by establishing learning events that are within the zone and then providing the right amount and kind of assistance, or scaffolding, to support learning.

One implication for children's literature and teaching noted earlier is for classrooms to be communities of learners in which readers, through discourse of all types but especially language and discussion, collaboratively build shared understandings about the texts they read. Another implication related to the zone of proximal development is the idea of teachable moments. These are the times when teachers can step in and help children reach new understanding by asking the right questions or offering information to build on the present insights that children share.

Nodelman and Reimer (2003) raise objections about the validity of child development theories, arguing that the whole concept of the nature of childhood is part of our society's ideology. As evidence they note that our views about children and their literature have changed over the centuries, so "what people now take for granted about them is not necessarily the complete or the only truth" (p. 85). In particular, they point out that any generalizations about children's literature based upon these theories (since they believe that the theories tend to portray all children in any given state as alike) "imply the degree to which people assume that all children live the comfortable, protected lives of white, middle-class North Americans" (p. 90), presumably lives similar to those of the children studied by the theorists. They also argue that the theories underestimate the potential of children to understand and discuss books that may be deemed too difficult for their cognitive level and, finally, that the theories are premised upon the idea that cognition is "evolutionary" and "privilege" adultlike over childlike thinking—all of which "represents an effort by adults to colonize children" (p. 97).

Nevertheless, Nodelman and Reimer (2003) also acknowledge that "the generalized children of ideological assumptions [namely, child development theories] are often the implied readers of texts written for children" (p. 95). These readers are ones suggested by a text's content and the way it is written, "the role [it] implies *and* invites a reader to take on" (p. 17). This concept, then, would argue for adults' need to know something about the match between the implied reader and what is known about children.

Imperfect and incomplete as child development theories may be, they and our knowledge of real child readers are the best guide to that match. Clearly, no single theory explains everything about children's development—and new ones will refine our present understanding—but the theories taken together provide the best current means to inform our thinking.

Children's Books Cited:
An Annotated List

Key to interest levels:

PK (preschool-kindergarten)

P (primary, grades 1–3)

I (intermediate, grades 4–5)

A (advanced, grades 6+)

Agard, John, & Nichols, Grace. (1995). *No hickory, no dickory, no dock: Caribbean nursery rhymes.* Illus. Cynthia Jabar. Cambridge, MA: Candlewick. (PK/P)
> *This collection of nursery rhymes and chants captures well the rhythms and dialect of the authors' native West Indies.*

Alexander, Lloyd. (1964). *The book of three.* New York: Holt, Rinehart and Winston. (I/A)
> *Taran is an assistant pig-keeper who longs to be a hero in the mythical kingdom of Prydain. He gets his wish for adventure and learns the true meaning of heroism along with a motley group of companions on a quest away from home and back again through a struggle between good and evil and a test that involve magic and transformation.*

Arnold, Caroline. (1997). *Hawk highway in the sky: Watching raptor migration.* Photo. Robert Kruidenier. San Diego, CA: Gulliver/Harcourt. (P/I)
> *This informational book, with full-color photographs, describes various raptors and their migration patterns as observed from the Hawkwatch International site in Nevada.*

Babbitt, Natalie. (1975). *Tuck everlasting.* New York: Farrar, Straus & Giroux. (I/A)
> *Jesse Tuck and his family, who have already drunk the magic spring's water decades earlier and are thus forever frozen in their life cycles, "save" Winnie from the same fate by kidnapping her until she can understand the danger posed to her by the innocent-looking water. A sinister man in a yellow suit is not so*

easily controlled, however, and some life-and-death consequences ensue in this fantasy novel.

Base, Graeme. (1987). *Animalia.* New York: Harry N. Abrams. (PK/P)
   This elaborately illustrated book, originally published in Australia, provides a visual puzzle for each letter of the alphabet.

Beake, Lesley. (1993). *Song of Be.* New York: Holt. (A)
   Young Be and her mother, who are Namibian San (or Bushman) people, descendants of the earliest human inhabitants of southern Africa, travel to find and live with her grandfather, who works on a large White-owned farm in this realistic novel. The farmer's wife develops a close relationship with Be, giving her an education. However, Be's childish innocence is slowly erased as she uncovers secrets that are the legacy of Namibia's troubled past under South African apartheid rule.

Belton, Sandra. (1993). *From Miss Ida's porch.* Illus. Floyd Cooper. New York: Four Winds. (P/I)
   At dusk, the children in an African American neighborhood gather on Miss Ida's porch to hear their elders recount true stories about Marian Anderson and Duke Ellington in this illustrated story.

Bishop, Nic. (2002). *Backyard detective: Critters up close.* New York: Scholastic. (P/I)
   Seven stunning photographic collages show life-size animal habitats of 125 creatures. Every collage in this informational text is accompanied by field notes, and a picture index identifies the location of each creature.

Boling, Katharine. (2002). *New year be coming! A Gullah year.* Illus. Daniel Minter. Morton Grove, IL: Albert Whitman. (P/I)
   Boling uses the Gullah dialect of the southeastern U.S. coastal islands to depict a way of life through the yearly seasons. A glossary explains unfamiliar terms.

Bradby, Marie. (1995). *More than anything else.* Illus. Chris K. Soentpiet. New York: Orchard. (P)
   Growing up in West Virginia and working in the saltworks with his father and brother, young Booker T. Washington wants to learn to read "more than anything else" in this picture book portrayal.

Branley, Franklyn. (1985). *Flash, crash, rumble, and roll.* Illus. Barbara & Ed Emberley. New York: Crowell. (P)
   This Let's-Read-and-Find-Out Science Book describes, through basic text and simple pictures, how a thunderstorm develops and happens.

Branley, Franklyn. (1988). *Tornado alert.* Illus. Giulio Maestro. New York: Crowell. (P)
   Another Let's-Read-and-Find-Out Science Book, this one explains why and how tornadoes form and what to do when one occurs.

Brown, Margaret Wise. (1947). *Goodnight, moon.* Illus. Clement Hurd. New York: HarperCollins. (PK)

This classic, gentle picture book story depicts a young rabbit saying goodnight to everything inside its bedroom and outside the window.

Bruchac, Joseph. (1996). *Between earth & sky: Legends of Native American sacred places.* Illus. Thomas Locker. San Diego, CA: Harcourt. (P/I)
Through the device of an elder teaching his nephew, 10 Native American sacred places across North America are poetically evoked and dramatically illustrated. A map shows locations of the settings and names the Indian people who lived in each area.

Bruchac, Joseph. (2000). *Squanto's journey: The story of the first Thanksgiving.* Illus. Greg Shed. San Diego, CA: Silver Whistle/Harcourt. (P/I)
This factual account of the first Thanksgiving is presented from the first-person perspective of Squanto, the Patuxet Indian who mediated between the Native Americans and the Pilgrims and helped the newcomers to survive.

Bruchac, Joseph, & London, Jonathan. (1992). *Thirteen moons on turtle's back: A Native American year of moons.* Illus. Thomas Locker. New York: Philomel. (P/I)
Each free-verse poem in this collection is associated with one of the 13 moons and derived from the stories of a different Native American tribal nation.

Bunting, Eve. (1989). *The Wednesday surprise.* Illus. Donald Carrick. New York: Clarion. (P)
A young girl secretly teaches her illiterate grandmother how to read with her own picture books during their Wednesday evenings together.

Bunting, Eve. (1994). *Smoky night.* Illus. David Diaz. San Diego, CA: Harcourt. (P/I)
Inspired by the riots in Los Angeles, this Caldecott Award–winning picture book shows how young Daniel and his mother fearfully watch the looting and burning. Through the connection of their cats, they are able to find friendship with Mrs. Kim, their formerly hostile neighbor.

Burleigh, Robert. (1991). *Flight.* Illus. Mike Wimmer. New York: Putnam. (P/I)
This biographical picture book presents an account of Charles Lindbergh's famous solo transatlantic flight.

Busby, Peter. (2002). *First to fly: How Wilbur & Orville Wright invented the airplane.* Illus. David Craig. New York: Crown. (P/I)
This enlarged-format account of the Wright brothers' invention describes the process from their childhood through adult lives. Full-color paintings are complemented with period photographs and additional sidebar information.

Case, Dianne. (1995). *92 Queens Road.* New York: Farrar, Straus & Giroux. (I/A)
This semiautobiographical book recounts the experiences of a young mixed-race (known as "coloured" in South Africa) girl growing up in the 1960s under apartheid.

Cherry, Lynne. (1992). *A river ran wild: An environmental history.* Orlando, FL: Harcourt. (P/I)
This informational picture book recounts the history of changes in the Nashua River in New Hampshire and Massachusetts. Years of White settlers' encroachment and industrial waste transformed this idyllic setting into a polluted, dying

place until individuals, with the help of new laws, began a campaign to clean and return the river to its former beauty.

Cole, Joanna. (1989). *The Magic School Bus inside the human body.* Illus. Bruce Degen. New York: Scholastic. (P/I)
Part of the Magic School Bus series, this title describes the field trip Ms. Frizzle's class takes to a museum that ends up going inside a human body.

Collier, James Lincoln, & Collier, Christopher. (1974). *My brother Sam is dead.* Old Tappan, NJ: Macmillan. (A)
Told from the point of view of Sam's younger brother Tim, this historical novel describes the gritty reality of the Revolutionary War's impact on a Connecticut village and the tragedy of Sam's execution after he joins the rebels and is accused of stealing cattle.

Conrad, Pam. (1995). *Call me Ahnighito.* Ill. Richard Egielski. New York: HarperCollins. (I)
This informational narrative revolves around a meteorite discovered in Greenland and christened by the Robert Peary expedition in 1897.

Cooney, Barbara. (1982). *Miss Rumphius.* New York: Viking. (P/I)
Alice Rumphius grows up in a New England seaport, travels the world, returns to live by the sea, and finds a way to make the world more beautiful in this picture book.

Curtis, Christopher Paul. (1995). *The Watsons go to Birmingham—1963.* New York: Delacorte. (I/A)
In 1963, the Watson family decides to leave Flint, Michigan, to travel south to visit Grandma in Birmingham, Alabama, after the parents think that older son Byron is becoming too delinquent. Told from the point of view of the younger son Kenny, this novel changes sharply from sidesplitting hilarity to posttraumatic pain following the family's encounter with a historically accurate church bombing carried out by White racists.

Daly, Niki. (1985). *Not so fast, Songololo.* London: Frances Lincoln. (PK/P)
In this South African picture book, young Songololo accompanies his gogo (grandmother) to the city to shop. Although she has little money, Gogo finds enough to buy her grandson a pair of new, bright red tackies (sneakers).

Daly, Niki. (2003). *Once upon a time.* New York: Farrar, Straus & Giroux. (P/I)
In another picture book from South Africa, Sarie dreads going to school because she struggles with reading aloud. However, a neighbor, Ou Missus, tells Sarie stories and helps her practice reading an old copy of Cinderella *until one day Sarie is able to demonstrate her mastery in class.*

Demi. (1997). *One grain of rice: A mathematical folktale.* New York: Scholastic. (P/I)
In this retelling from India, a girl cleverly uses a reward she receives from the raja to get the rice he refuses to share with the hungry villagers. By asking for one grain of rice to be doubled every day, in 30 days Rani has obtained more

than a billion grains—enough for everyone, including the raja. A mathemati-
cal chart tallies the number of rice grains Rani receives each day.

Dewey, Jennifer. (1994). *Wildlife rescue: The work of Dr. Kathleen Ramsay*. Photo. Don McCarter. Honesdale, PA: Boyds Mills. (P/I)

This informational book recounts how veterinarian Dr. Ramsay rehabilitates
sick and injured animals at the Wildlife Center in New Mexico so they can return
to and survive in their natural habitats.

DiCamillo, Kate. (2003). *The tale of Despereaux*. Illus. Timothy Basil Ering. Cambridge, MA: Candlewick. (I)

In this Newbery Award–winning fantasy, Despereaux, an exceptional mouse,
is born in a castle with a princess named Pea, whom he comes to love. She is
imperiled, however, by Miggory Sow, a serving girl, who conspires with the
evil rat Roscuro to usurp Pea's position. Despereaux embarks on an adven-
ture to save Pea.

Ehlert, Lois. (1990). *Feathers for lunch*. Orlando, FL: Harcourt. (PK/P)

In this elongated-format picture book, a cat is on the hunt for a wild lunch,
but all the birds he tries to catch know how to elude him. A glossary at the end
provides information about the specific birds mentioned.

Ehlert, Lois. (1995). *Snowballs*. New York: Scholastic. (PK)

This picture book uses simple text and large collage illustrations to show the
snow family that children create. To view the full length of each snow statue,
the book must be turned sideways.

Falconer, Ian. (2000). *Olivia*. New York: Scholastic. (PK/P)

Olivia, a lovable young pig, engages in nonstop childlike activity that wears
out everyone else in this picture book.

Farmer, Nancy. (1996). *A girl named Disaster*. New York: Orchard. (A)

Set in Mozambique, this novel portrays the journey of Nhamo, an 11-year-old
Shona girl, as she flees her village after her mother dies and before an impend-
ing forced marriage to search for her father's relatives in Zimbabwe. Along
the way, Nhamo enters the spirit realm of her ancestors and faces many dan-
gers from animals, people, and the elements of nature.

Flack, Marjorie. (1933). *The story about Ping*. Illus. Kurt Weise. New York: Viking. (PK)

This classic picture book recounts a young duck's adventures when, at the end
of the day, he misses boarding his home boat on the Yangtze River and is left
behind. In the end, he returns safely and somewhat wiser to his duck family
and relatives.

Fleming, Denise. (1992). *Lunch*. New York: Henry Holt. (PK)

Similar to Eric Carle's The Very Hungry Caterpillar (*New York, Philomel,*
1981), this picture book describes a very hungry mouse that eats eight fruits
and vegetables for lunch, one at a time. Each double-page spread gives a sneak
peak at the next food he will eat.

Fleming, Denise. (1996). *Where once there was a wood*. New York: Henry Holt. (PK/P)

> *Lyrical text and bright pulp paintings depict the encroachment by a suburban housing development into woods filled with wildlife. At the end of this picture book, the author describes how to create welcoming habitats for plants and animals.*

Fleming, Denise. (2002). *Alphabet under construction*. New York: Henry Holt. (PK/P)

> *In this picture book, a mouse constructs each letter of the alphabet with a verb that begins with that letter.*

Franklin, Kristine L., & McGirr, Nancy (Eds.). (1995). *Out of the dump: Writings and photographs by children from Guatemala*. New York: Lothrop, Lee & Shepard. (I/A)

> *Black-and-white photographs taken by children and their original essays show the everyday lives of dump dwellers in Guatemala City. Photographer Nancy McGirr started this project in 1991; the proceeds from it go toward the children's education.*

Freedman, Russell. (1994). *Kids at work: Lewis Hine and the crusade against child labor*. New York: Clarion. (I/A)

> *Lewis Hine's photographs accompany Freedman's informational text about Hine's dedication to changing American child labor practices in the early 20th century.*

Fritz, Jean. (1973). *And then what happened, Paul Revere?* Illus. Margot Tomes. New York: Putnam. (P/I)

> *One of Fritz's "question biographies," this lively account tells about not only Revere's famous ride but also the many activities that occupied his daily life.*

Fritz, Jean. (1989). *The great little Madison*. New York: Putnam. (I/A)

> *This full-length biography of James Madison includes maps, copies of paintings from the era, and photographs of actual objects to present the life of one of the founders of the United States and its fourth president.*

Gallaz, Christophe, & Innocenti, Roberto. (1985). *Rose Blanche*. Trans. Martha Coventry & Richard Graglia. Mankato, MN: Creative Education. (P/I)

> *In this picture book from France, Rose Blanche, a schoolgirl in Germany when the Nazis come to power, witnesses a boy trying to escape from a military convoy that stops briefly in her town and how harshly he is treated when he is quickly caught. Curious, she follows the truck out of town to a clearing in the forest where she finds a prison camp filled with starving people. After that, she regularly visits the camp, bringing food to the Jewish inmates. As the war is ending, she finds the camp deserted one day; she apparently is shot by retreating German soldiers.*

Gantos, Jack. (1994). *Heads or tails*. New York: Farrar, Straus & Giroux. (I/A)

> *This episodic novel is the first in a series about the everyday triumphs and trials of Jack Henry. In this volume, he is in sixth grade and living in Florida in the 1960s.*

Gantos, Jack. (1995). *Jack's new power.* New York: Farrar, Straus & Giroux. (I/A)
Now 13, Jack has moved with his family to the Caribbean, where his experiences are chronicled in his diary.

Gantos, Jack. (1997). *Jack's black book.* New York: Farrar, Straus & Giroux. (I/A)
Jack returns to Florida at the end of seventh grade and decides to write a novel, in his quest to become a writer.

Gantos, Jack. (1999). *Jack on the tracks.* New York: Farrar, Straus & Giroux. (I/A)
This series prequel, which returns Jack to fifth grade when his family moves from North Carolina to Florida, recounts his travails with and perspective on life and family.

Garay, Luis. (1997). *Pedrito's day.* New York: Orchard. (P)
This picture book portrays a Central American boy, whose father has gone north to work, trying to save money he earns by shining shoes to buy a bicycle.

George, Jean Craighead. (1972). *Julie of the wolves.* New York: HarperCollins. (A)
In this Newbery Award–winning novel set in Alaska, Julie/Miyax runs away from a traditional arranged marriage and becomes lost on the vast Arctic tundra. She survives by gaining acceptance from a pack of wolves until she is able to make her way to the village where her father lives. What she finds there, however, forces her to come to terms with contemporary realities.

George, Jean Craighead. (1993). *The first Thanksgiving.* Illus. Thomas Locker. New York: Philomel. (P/I)
This informational book presents the arrival of the Pilgrims and their celebration of survival, with the help of Squanto and the Massasoit Indians, after the first successful harvest.

George, Jean Craighead. (1995). *Everglades.* Illus. Wendell Minor. New York: HarperCollins. (P/I)
The evolution of an endangered ecosystem is presented from the perspective of a Seminole storyteller in this informational book.

Giff, Patricia Reilly. (2002). *Pictures of Hollis Woods.* New York: Wendy Lamb/ Random House. (I/A)
In this contemporary novel, 12-year-old Hollis Woods was abandoned as a baby and lived in foster homes her whole life. When she runs away from a loving family who wants to adopt her, she faces more complications from Social Services, which suspects that the elderly woman with whom she is placed is becoming too forgetful to properly care for Hollis.

Gollub, Matthew. (1998). *Cool melons—turn to frogs!* Illus. Kazuko G. Stone. Calligraphy by Keiko Smith. New York: Lee & Low. (P/I/A)
This combination of poetry and biography presents the life and writing of the 18th-century Japanese haiku poet Issa.

Greenfeld, Howard. (1993). *Hidden children.* New York: Ticknor & Fields. (I/A)
For this informational book, Greenfeld interviews 13 Jewish adults who were hidden as children by non-Jews and survived the Holocaust.

Gregorowski, Christopher. (2000). *Fly, eagle, fly!* Illus. Niki Daly. New York: McElderry. (P/I)

> *Attributed to the 19th-century Ghanaian scholar Dr. James Kwegyir Aggrey, this is the story of a farmer who discovers a lost eagle chick, which he brings home and raises among his chickens. Surrounded by these creatures, the eagle grows up thinking it, too, is a chicken, until a friend of the farmer recognizes its true nature. After several unsuccessful attempts, the friend persuades the eagle to fly as it was meant to do. A foreword by South African Archbishop Desmond Tutu and Niki Daly's illustrator's note both reinforce the story's metaphor for the newly liberated people of South Africa.*

Grimes, Nikki. (2001). *A pocketful of poems.* Illus. Javaka Steptoe. New York: Clarion. (P/I)

> *Tiana's city life is celebrated in this collection of free verse and haiku poems, accompanied by Steptoe's collage illustrations.*

Hall, Donald. (1979). *Ox-cart man.* Illus. Barbara Cooney. New York: Viking. (P/I)

> *This Caldecott Award–winning informational picture book portrays the yearly cycle of a New England pioneer family's life.*

Hamilton, Virginia. (1985, 2004). *The people could fly: The picture book.* Illus. Leo and Diane Dillon. New York: Knopf. (P/I)

> *New illustrations complement this solo folktale about American Black slaves who flew up in the air to freedom when they could no longer bear their misery.*

Hamilton, Virginia. (1993). *Many thousand gone: African Americans from slavery to freedom.* Illus. Leo and Diane Dillon. New York: Knopf. (P/I/A)

> *The stories of individual African Americans from the earliest days of slavery through their emancipation are presented in this informational book.*

Hirsch, Robin. (2002). *FEG: Ridiculous ~~stupid~~ poems for intelligent children.* Illus. Ha. Boston: Little, Brown. (P/I/A)

> *This witty collection of poems, accompanied by extensive notes, playfully explores word meanings and language forms and terms.*

Hoestlandt, Jo. (1993). *Star of fear, star of hope.* Trans. Mark Polizzotti. Illus. Johanna Kang. New York: Walker. (P/I)

> *In this picture book from France, Helen, who narrates the story as an old woman, sadly remembers when she was angry as a girl that her best friend, Lydia, suddenly departed Helen's birthday sleepover because of a middle-of-the-night alarm about a roundup of Jews. Helen hopes that Lydia somehow managed to survive the Holocaust, became a grandma like her, reads the story, and calls to reestablish their friendship.*

Houston, Gloria. (1992). *My great-aunt Arizona.* Illus. Susan Condie Lamb. New York: HarperCollins. (P/I)

> *This loving picture book tribute presents Arizona, who was born and raised in Appalachia and grew up to become a teacher who passed on her love for reading to generations of students.*

Hutchins, Pat. (1968). *Rosie's walk*. New York: Simon & Schuster. (PK)
   When Rosie the hen goes for a walk, she is chased all around the farm by a fox who never quite manages to nab the innocent chicken in this picture book.
Keats, Ezra Jack. (1962). *The snowy day*. New York: Viking. (PK/P)
   This picture book depicts young Peter's magical day spent playing in fresh snow.
Kraus, Robert. (1971). *Leo the late bloomer*. Illus. Jose Aruego. New York: HarperCollins. (PK)
   Leo, a young tiger, cannot do anything as well as the other young animals in this picture book. His father wonders when Leo will bloom, but his mother tells his father not to worry.
Kurtz, Jane. (1997). *Trouble*. Illus. Durga Bernhard. Orlando, FL: Harcourt. (P/I)
   Trouble happens in this folktale originating from Eritrea when a young boy has the responsibility of tending his family's goats, but they always end up in someone's garden. Tekleh's father gives him a gebeta board game to keep him out of trouble. When Tekleh sets off the next day with the goats and gebeta board, one thing leads to another, but in the end, Tekleh, the goats, and a different gebeta board successfully return home.
Lauber, Patricia. (1986). *Volcano: The eruption and healing of Mount St. Helens*. New York: Bradbury. (P/I/A)
   This nonfiction account portrays the cycle of destruction and rebirth of a volcano eruption.
Lauber, Patricia. (1996). *Hurricanes: Earth's mightiest storms*. New York: Scholastic. (I/A)
   The worst hurricanes of the 20th century are recounted through informational text, photographs, maps, and diagrams.
L'Engle, Madeleine. (1962). *A wrinkle in time*. New York: Farrar, Straus & Giroux. (I/A)
   In this the science fantasy quest, Meg Murry, her brother Charles Wallace, and her friend Calvin search for Meg's scientist father, who has disappeared in space. Many adventures later, they find him being held prisoner on another planet, rescue him from evil forces, and safely return to Earth together.
Lester, Julius. (1998). *From slave ship to freedom road*. Illus. Rod Brown. New York: Dial. (I/A)
   Brown's paintings inspired Lester's informational text to present various perspectives of African Americans' journey from slavery to freedom.
Levenson, George. (1999). *Pumpkin circle*. Berkeley, CA: Tricycle. (PK/P)
   This photoessay presents the yearly life cycle of pumpkins.
Lewis, J. Patrick. (2001). *Good mousekeeping and other animal home poems*. Illus. Lisa Desimini. New York: Atheneum. (P/I)
   These humorous verses use puns and other clever word combinations to describe possible animal homes.

Lionni, Leo. (1967). *Frederick.* New York: Knopf. (PK/P)
>   *While Frederick's field mice family diligently collects food and supplies for the winter in this picture book, Frederick spends his time gathering rays of the sun, warm colors, and words that he shares to enrich their lives in the dead of winter.*

Locker, Thomas. (1997). *Water dance.* San Diego, CA: Harcourt. (P/I)
>   *Free-verse text and oil-paint illustrations depict the different forms of water. Scientific explanations are provided at the end.*

Locker, Thomas. (2000). *Cloud dance.* San Diego, CA: Harcourt. (P/I)
>   *Similar in format to Locker's* Water Dance, *this informational book shows the different appearances of clouds.*

Locker, Thomas. (2001). *Mountain dance.* San Diego, CA: Harcourt. (P/I)
>   *Also similar in format to Locker's* Water Dance, *and to his* Cloud Dance, *this informational book describes different types of mountains and how they were created.*

Locker, Thomas, & Christiansen, Candace. (1995). *Sky tree: Seeing science through art.* New York: HarperCollins. (P/I)
>   *This informational book combines visual and scientific changes of a single tree throughout a year's cycle.*

Lowry, Lois. (1993). *The giver.* New York: Houghton Mifflin. (A)
>   *This futuristic novel (winner of the Newbery medal) is set in a perfect community in which all differences are eliminated and no one can remember any other kind of life. Jonas, as he turns 12 years old, is assigned his adult role to become the new Receiver of memories for the community and, in the process, becomes increasingly aware of the lies and hypocrisies all around him. When he discovers what will happen to Gabriel, the infant who comes to live temporarily with his family, Jonas decides to take drastic action.*

Luenn, Nancy. (1998). *A gift for Abuelita: Celebrating the Day of the Dead/Un regalo para Abuelita: En celebración del Día de los Muertos.* Illus. Robert Chapman. Flagstaff, AZ: Rising Moon. (P/I)
>   *This bilingual picture book about the Mexican celebration of the Day of the Dead portrays the close, loving relationship between a young girl and her grandmother. When Abuelita dies, Rosita misses her terribly, and her grandfather teaches Rosita how to express her loss by creating a special gift for Abuelita to place on the family altar to honor their dead loved ones.*

Macauley, David. (1991). *Black and white.* New York: Putnam. (P/I/A)
>   *This Caldecott Award–winning picture book appears to contain four narratives depicted on each spread, but read in multiple directions. They may be four parts of a fifth metastory, which is determined by the reader's choices.*

MacLachlan, Patricia. (1985). *Sarah, plain and tall.* New York: Harper & Row. (I)
>   *A Newbery Award–winning novella, this historical fiction story tells how Sarah comes as a mail-order bride from Maine to live with two children and their father on their prairie homestead. Told from the perspective of Anna, the elder*

child, readers learn how she and her younger brother, Caleb, feel about having a new mother and their hopes that Sarah will stay.

Madrigal, Antonio Hernández. (1999). *Erandi's braids.* Illus. Tomie dePaola. New York: Putnam. (P/I)

> In this picture book, Erandi, a young Mexican girl, helps her mother earn enough money for a new fishing net, for their work, and a new doll by selling her long, beautiful braids to the hair buyer.

Martin, Jacqueline Briggs. (1998). *Snowflake Bentley.* Illus. Mary Azarian. New York: Scholastic. (P/I)

> This Caldecott Medal picture book biography presents the life of Wilson Bentley, who studied snowflakes and developed the technique of microphotography to show the shapes of snow crystals. The main narrative is accompanied by text sidebars with additional facts.

Mayer, Mercer. (1968). *There's a nightmare in my closet.* New York: Dial. (PK/P)

> A young boy conquers and then comforts a nightmare that used to be in his closet in this reassuring picture book.

McCloskey, Robert. (1957). *Time of wonder.* New York: Viking. (PK/P)

> This classic picture book describes a beautiful and awe-inspiring late-summer storm on an island off the coast of Maine.

McKay, Hilary. (2002). *Saffy's angel.* New York: McElderry. (I/A)

> Saffy feels upset and displaced when she accidentally discovers that she is adopted. This award-winning contemporary novel is set in England.

McKissack, Patricia. (1986). *Flossie and the fox.* Illus. Rachel Isadora. New York: Dial. (PK/P)

> In this retelling from McKissack's childhood, Flossie is a young girl sent by her Big Mama to carry a basket of eggs to a neighbor. To get there, Flossie takes a shortcut through the woods, where she encounters a fox who hungrily eyes her basket of eggs while trying to convince her that he is, indeed, a fox.

McKissack, Patricia C., & McKissack, Fredrick L. (1994). *Christmas in the big house, Christmas in the quarters.* Illus. John Thompson. New York: Scholastic. (P/I)

> Two divergent perspectives—the slaves' and the owners'—on Christmas preparations and celebration on a Virginia plantation just before the Civil War are presented in this nonfiction narrative.

McPhail, David. (1987). *Fix-it!* New York: Puffin. (PK)

> When the television doesn't work, Emma, a young bear, demands that her parents fix it until her mother reads her a book—like this picture book.

McPhail, David. (1997). *Edward and the pirates.* New York: Scholastic. (PK/P)

> In this picture book, young Edward loves to read adventure tales. One about buried treasure becomes so real that pirates storm his bedroom at night and demand to see his book. His mother (a.k.a. Joan of Arc) and his father (a.k.a. Robin Hood) save him from the threatening pirates, who meekly agree to listen as Edward reads the story aloud to them.

Meyer, Carolyn. (1996). *Gideon's people*. San Diego: Harcourt Brace. (A)
  This work of historical fiction is set in early 20th-century Lancaster County,
  Pennsylvania. Isaac, an Orthodox Jewish boy, travels with his peddler father
  to visit the Amish farms nearby. An accident forces Isaac to remain with an
  Amish family to heal for a period of time. While there, Isaac learns why the
  teenage son Gideon finally decides he needs to leave home.
Minor, Wendell. (1998). *Grand Canyon: Exploring a natural wonder*. New York:
Scholastic. (P/I)
  This illustrated essay portrays the artist's examination of a natural wonder from
  many perspectives.
Mollel, Tololwa M. (1999). *My rows and piles of coins*. Illus. E. B. Lewis. New York:
Clarion. (P/I)
  In this picture book, Saruni, a Tanzanian boy, saves money he earns, by help-
  ing his mother on market day, for a bicycle that he then uses to transport more
  fruit and vegetables to market.
Mora, Pat. (1996). *Confetti: Poems for children*. Illus. Enrique O. Sanchez. New
York: Lee & Low. (P/I)
  See Pat Mora, 2006, for annotation.
Mora, Pat. (2005). *Doña Flor: A tall tale about a giant woman with a great big*
heart. Illus. Raul Colón. New York: Knopf.
Mora, Pat. (2005). *Doña Flor: Un cuento de una mujer gigante con un gran corazón*.
Illus. Raul Colón. New York: Dragonfly. (PK/P/I)
  These two picture books are the English and Spanish versions of an original
  tall tale set in the southwestern United States about a giant woman who be-
  friends the village children and protects them when they hear a frightening,
  mysterious noise.
Mora, Pat. (2006). *Confeti: Poemas para niños*. Illus. Enrique O. Sanchez. Trans.
Queta Fernández & Pat Mora. New York: Lee & Low. (P/I)
  The English edition published in 1996 and the 2006 Spanish translation of this
  poetry collection celebrate the imagination and everyday experiences of young
  children.
Murphy, Jim. (2000). *Blizzard: The storm that changed America*. New York: Scholastic. (I/A)
  The blizzard of 1888 that paralyzed the northeastern United States is detailed
  in this informational book.
Naidoo, Beverley. (1985). *Journey to Jo'burg*. London: Longman. (I/A)
  This novel, set in apartheid South Africa, recounts the 300-kilometer jour-
  ney that a Black girl and her younger brother make on foot from their vil-
  lage to Johannesburg to find their mother, who works there as a domestic
  servant to a White family. Naledi and Tiro need to fetch her to tend to their
  seriously ill baby sister, whom they have left in the care of their grandmother.
  All safely return together to the village and baby Dineo gets well, but the
  journey is more than a physical trip, as Naledi also learns many hard truths

that she did not know before about the reality of the Black struggle under apartheid.

Naidoo, Beverley. (1990). *Chain of fire.* New York: HarperCollins. (A)

A sequel to Journey to Jo'burg, *this novel depicts Naledi (now age 13) as a student who becomes involved in the struggle against the apartheid South African government's forced removal of Blacks from the town where they have lived all their lives. She and a group of friends organize demonstrations to resist this atrocity and initiate a chain of events that lead to an inevitable conclusion.*

Naylor, Phyllis Reynolds. (1991). *Shiloh.* New York: Simon & Schuster. (I)

This Newbery Medal–winning contemporary realistic novel set in West Virginia tells how 11-year-old Marty one day finds a beagle that belongs to an abusive neighbor. His parents say he must return the dog, but Marty secretly decides to save Shiloh.

Olaleye, Isaac. (2001). *Bicycles for rent!* Illus. Chris Demarest. New York: Orchard. (P/I)

A young Nigerian, Lateef, yearns for his own bicycle in this picture book. He makes money by collecting and selling firewood and mushrooms until he saves enough to rent and eventually own one.

Old, Wendie C. (2002). *To fly: The story of the Wright brothers.* Illus. Robert Andrew Parker. New York: Clarion. (P/I)

This biographical account highlights the Wright brothers' fascination with flight from their boyhood playful experiments to their successful takeoff in 1903.

Onyefulu, Ifeoma. (1996). *Ogbo: Sharing life in an African village.* San Diego, CA: Gulliver/Harcourt. (P/I)

This photoessay shows the people, activities, and surroundings that make up a contemporary Nigerian village.

Orlev, Uri. (1984). *The island on Bird Street.* Trans. Hillel Halkin. Boston: Houghton Mifflin. (I/A)

This award-winning historical novel from Israel depicts a boy's survival alone while waiting for his father to return to the Jewish ghetto of Warsaw, Poland, during the Holocaust.

Paterson, Katherine. (1977). *Bridge to Terabithia.* New York: Harper & Row. (I/A)

In this Newbery Award–winning contemporary novel, Jess's greatest dream is to be the fastest runner in the fifth grade—until he meets his new neighbor, Leslie, who opens his rural world to a whole new set of imagined possibilities. Jess's artistic talent also is recognized by Miss Edmunds, his art teacher, and the confidence he gains from both relationships helps Jess deal with the loss and pain of Leslie's tragic death.

Paulsen, Gary. (1987). *Hatchet.* New York: Atheneum. (A)

When Brian's airplane, in which he is the only passenger, crashes in the Canadian wilderness after the pilot dies of a heart attack, the 13-year-old is just beginning his adventure in this realistic contemporary novel, as he learns to survive alone with only the hatchet his mother had given him.

Piper, Watty. (1930/1978). *The little engine that could.* Illus. George Hauman & Doris Hauman. New York: Grosset & Dunlap. (PK)
   This classic picture book presents the power of positive thinking in the form of a little engine that decides to try to pull the train of toys over a tall mountain when other bigger and stronger engines say they cannot do it.

Platt, Richard. (1999). *Castle diary: The journal of Tobias Burgess, Page.* Illus. Chris Riddell. Cambridge, MA: Candlewick. (I/A)
   This oversized nonfiction book, enhanced by detailed illustrations, presents the daily life of a fictional page in a 13th-century European castle. Beyond the imaginary diary, further information is provided in explanatory notes to the reader.

Polacco, Patricia. (1998). *Thank you, Mr. Falker.* New York: Philomel. (P/I)
   Trisha (a.k.a. the author) tells the poignant story of her struggles with learning to read in this picture book.

Potter, Beatrice. (1902). *The tale of Peter Rabbit.* New York: Warne. (PK)
   This classic miniature picture book relates the narrative of Peter, a young rabbit, who, in spite of his mother's stern warnings, heads straight for Mr. McGregor's garden to feast on the delicious things growing there. Narrowly escaping a fate of becoming the farmer's rabbit pie, Peter is sent to bed early with medicine, instead of supper.

Rathman, Peggy. (1995). *Officer Buckle and Gloria.* New York: Scholastic. (P/I)
   In this Caldecott Award–winning picture book, Officer Buckle's boring safety lectures at schools are enlivened by the addition of a police dog named Gloria, who, unbeknownst to Officer Buckle, cleverly dramatizes his safety tips behind his back.

Ringgold, Faith. (1999). *If a bus could talk: The story of Rosa Parks.* New York: Simon & Schuster. (P/I)
   Rosa Parks's historic ride is recounted by a personified bus to a fictional girl on her way to school in this picture book.

Ryan, Pam Muñoz. (2004). *Becoming Naomi León.* New York: Scholastic. (I/A)
   This contemporary novel portrays the conflicted feelings that Naomi and her brother, Owen, feel when, after years of living with their great-grandmother, their mother suddenly reappears. Once the children discover their mother's true motives, they and Gram flee to search for the children's father in Mexico.

Sachar, Louis. (1998). *Holes.* New York: Farrar, Straus & Giroux. (I/A)
   This Newbery Award–winning magic realism novel presents the ill-fated Stanley Yelnats, who is mistakenly sentenced to the juvenile detention Camp Green Lake, where boys spend all their time digging holes in the middle of a dried-up lake. Stanley learns much more than character improvement when he uncovers the real purpose of the camp.

Schertle, Alice. (1995). *Down the road.* Illus. E. B. Lewis. Orlando, FL: Harcourt. (PK/P)

This picture book portrays a young girl named Hetty, who is allowed by her parents one day to walk down the road from her home by herself to get eggs from Mr. Birdie's store. On the return home, the egg basket tips when Hetty reaches for some tempting apples in a tree. The eggs are broken and she climbs into the tree to avoid going home, but her parents, one at a time, find her, join her in the tree, and finally walk home with her together with no eggs but plenty of apples.

Schertle, Alice. (2002). *All you need for a snowman.* Illus. Barbara Lavallee. San Diego, CA: Harcourt. (PK/P)

This picture book poem is a celebration of creating a snowman.

Schwartz, David M. (1999). *On beyond a million: An amazing math journey.* Illus. Paul Meisel. New York: Doubleday. (P/I)

Professor X teaches students how to use exponential numbers to count popcorn kernels by exponents of 10 in this informational narrative.

Sendak, Maurice. (1963). *Where the Wild Things are.* New York: HarperCollins. (PK/P)

When Max pretends to be a Wild Thing, his mother sends him to his room without his supper. There Max sails off to the land of the Wild Things, where he rules until he smells good things to eat and returns home to find his supper waiting for him in this Caldecott Medal picture book.

Sendak, Maurice. (1993). *We are all in the dumps with Jack and Guy: Two nursery rhymes with pictures.* New York: HarperCollins. (P/I/A)

Two nursery rhymes are woven into a dark fable of poverty, greed, and salvation with numerous allusions to events and realities of the 20th century.

Simon, Seymour. (1989). *Whales.* New York: HarperCollins. (P/I)

This informational text presents facts accompanied by striking color photographs of several whale species.

Sís, Peter. (1998). *Tibet through the red box.* New York: Farrar, Straus & Giroux. (I/A)

Through his own adult memories and his father's diary, the author reconstructs in this oversized picture book the period when his father, a Czech filmmaker, was lost in Tibet for several years.

Sisulu, Eleanor Batezat. (1996). *The day Gogo went to vote.* Illus. Sharon Wilson. Boston: Little, Brown. (P/I)

Young Thembi accompanies her great-grandmother to vote in the first multiracial election in South Africa in 1994 in this picture book account.

Steig, William. (1969). *Sylvester and the magic pebble.* New York: Simon & Schuster. (PK/P)

This picture book is the tale of a young donkey that finds a magic pebble, which grants him any wish he makes. However, when he is confronted by a lion, Sylvester foolishly wishes to change into a rock, in which condition he remains until nearly a year later, when a lucky circumstance allows him to be transformed back into a donkey and restored to his loving parents.

Steig, William. (1971). *Amos & Boris*. New York: Farrar, Straus & Giroux. (P/I)
> *Amos, a mouse, builds himself a boat and embarks on an adventure on the high seas in this picture book. A careless mistake lands him in the ocean and unable to reach his boat. Boris, a whale, happens along, saves Amos, and takes him safely home. Years later, after a hurricane beaches Boris, Amos is able to return the favor.*

Swanson, Diane. (1994). *Safari beneath the sea: The wonder world of the north Pacific coast*. Photo. Royal British Columbia Museum. San Francisco: Sierra Club. (P/I)
> *Informational text and color photography take readers on an underwater journey through a visual wonderland of close-up views of strange and marvelous sea creatures and plant life.*

Sweeney, Joan. (2000). *Me counting time: From seconds to centuries*. Illus. Annette Cable. New York: Crown. (P/I)
> *This informational book depicts in a lighthearted way the concepts of how time is marked.*

Taylor, Mildred D. (1976). *Roll of thunder, hear my cry*. New York: Dial. (I/A)
> *Based on her own family stories, this award-winning fictional account presents the Logan family's experiences during the Depression in Mississippi from the perspective of the spirited, 9-year-old Cassie. Although her parents had shielded her from much racist bigotry, in one year she loses her innocence about the ugly facts of life for Blacks at that time in the American South.*

Taylor, Mildred D. (1995). *The well*. New York: Dial. (I/A)
> *This historical novella, also based on Taylor's family history, recounts what happens when the Logan family shares their well water with all their neighbors, Black and White alike, yet bad blood remains between Hammer and the White Simms brothers.*

Turkington, Nola, & Daly, Niki. (1996). *The dancer*. Illus. Niki Daly. Cape Town, South Africa: Human & Rousseau. (P/I)
> *This southern African picture book tells how young Bau dances the stories of her San people and creates new dances for what she experiences. When a time of terrible drought comes, Bau dances with the rainbull to make him give rain. The illustration style borrows from prehistoric San rock paintings.*

Waber, Bernard. (1972). *Ira sleeps over*. Boston: Houghton Mifflin. (PK/P)
> *In this picture book, young Ira is afraid to bring his teddy bear when he spends the night for the first time at his friend's house.*

Waldman, Neil. (2001). *They came from the Bronx: How the buffalo were saved from extinction*. Honesdale, PA: Boyds Mills. (P/I)
> *Through informational text and illustrations, Waldman intertwines the survival of both American bison and the Comanche Indian culture.*

Wesley, Valerie. (1997). *Freedom's gift: A Juneteenth story*. Illus. Sharon Wilson. New York: Simon & Schuster. (P/I)
> *This picture book commemorates, through the stories of Great-Great Aunt Marshall to two young cousins, the African American celebration of June 19, 1865, when slaves in Texas learned about their freedom.*

White, E. B. (1952). *Charlotte's web*. Illus. Garth Williams. New York: HarperCollins. (P/I)
> This classic novel about the lovable runt pig Wilbur shows how the clever spider Charlotte devises a way to save him from becoming bacon.

White, Ruth. (2004). *Buttermilk Hill*. New York: Farrar, Straus & Giroux. (I/A)
> Piper Woods gradually discovers her talent for writing poetry as a way to deal with her parents' divorce and the mystery of her friend's life. This novel is set in North Carolina in the 1970s.

Wick, Walter. (2002). *Can you see what I see? Picture puzzles to search and solve*. New York: Scholastic. (P/I)
> This playful nonfiction book presents a series of artfully arranged puzzles of visual problems and illusions in photographic arrangements of real objects with clues provided in accompanying text.

Wiesner, David. (2001). *The three pigs*. New York: Clarion. (P/I)
> A Caldecott Award winner, this thoroughly postmodern rendition of the classic folktale defies conventions of traditional storytelling and illustration as the three pigs fly out of their story into other well-known tales.

Willems, Mo. (2004). *Knuffle Bunny*. New York: Hyperion. (PK/P)
> A very young Trixie is devastated when she and her daddy accidentally leave Knuffle Bunny at the Laundromat in this unusual mixed-media picture book.

Williams, Karen Lynn. (1998). *Painted dreams*. Illus. Catherine Stock. New York: Lothrop, Lee & Shepard. (P/I)
> This picture book presents Ti Marie's ambition to become an artist, but her family, living in Haiti, has no money to buy her paints, brushes, or canvas. When Ti Marie discovers some paint in the garbage, she creates brilliant murals on the wall behind her mother's market stall that attract many more paying customers.

Williams, Vera B. (1990). *"More, more, more," said the baby*. New York: Scholastic. (PK)
> Three small children are each playfully handled by a loving adult in this simple, repetitional picture book.

Woodson, Jacqueline. (1995). *From the notebooks of Melanin Sun*. New York: Blue Sky/Scholastic. (A)
> Thirteen-year-old Melanin Sun has a rough time dealing with his mother's same-sex relationship with a White woman and his dawning awareness of his own sexuality in this contemporary realistic novel.

Woodson, Jacqueline. (2003). *Locomotion*. New York: Putnam. (I/A)
> This contemporary novel presents Lonnie Collins Motion, an 11-year-old living with a foster mother, whose teacher persuades him to write about his life—losing his parents and being separated from his younger sister.

Yep, Laurence. (1975). *Dragonwings*. New York: Harper & Row. (I/A)
> This historical novel presents Moon Shadow's arrival in America and adjustment to San Francisco's Chinatown against the backdrop of the 1906

earthquake. His father's fascination and experiments with building a flying machine provide a metaphor for following one's dream.

Yorinks, Arthur. (1986). *Hey, Al.* Illus. Richard Egielski. New York: Farrar, Straus & Giroux. (P/I)

This picture book concerns a janitor who lives quietly with his dog, Eddie, in a one-room apartment in the city. To escape their humdrum existence, they are enticed by an exotic bird to a tropical island, where they eventually begin to morph into birds themselves. When they fly home in desperation at this unwelcome turn of events, Eddie flies too high and plunges into the sea. A happy ending leads to this piece of timeless wisdom: "Paradise lost is sometimes Heaven found" (unpaginated).

Yumoto, Kazumi. (1992). *The friends.* New York: Farrar, Straus & Giroux. (I/A)

Three boys spend the summer after grade 6 trying to satisfy their curiosity about death by spying on an elderly man who they are sure is dying. The old man, however, turns the tables on their pranks, wins their friendship, and teaches them some lessons about life. This contemporary Japanese novel conveys universal themes while portraying a specific culture.

Zelinsky, Paul O. (1997). *Rapunzel.* New York: Dutton. (P/I)

This Caldecott Award–winning retelling of the traditional fairy tale is beautifully illustrated in the Italian Renaissance painting style.

Zelinsky, Paul. (2002). *Knick-knack paddywhack!* New York: Dutton. (PK/P)

This movable-parts picture book makes the familiar counting song "This Old Man" highly interactive.

References

Allen, V. G. (1995). Children's literature, language development, and literacy. In M. R. Sorensen & B. A. Lehman (Eds.), *Teaching with children's books: Paths to literature-based instruction* (pp. 40–48). Urbana, IL: National Council of Teachers of English.

Anderson, R. A., Hiebert, E. H., Scott, J. A., & Wilkinson, I. A. G. (1985). *Becoming a nation of readers: The report of the Commission on Reading.* Champaign, IL: National Academy of Education, National Institute of Education, Center for the Study of Reading.

Applebee, A. (1978). *The child's concept of story: Ages two to 17.* Chicago: University of Chicago Press.

Appleyard, J. A. (1990). *Becoming a reader: The experience of fiction from adolescence to adulthood.* New York: Cambridge University Press.

Atwell, N. (1987). *In the middle: Writing, reading, and learning with adolescents.* Portsmouth, NH: Heinemann.

Baldick, C. (2004). *The concise dictionary of literary terms.* New York: Oxford University Press.

Barton, K. C., & Smith, L. A. (2000). Themes or motifs? Aiming for coherence through interdisciplinary outlines. *The Reading Teacher, 54,* 54–63.

Beach, J. D. (1993). Literacy through literature: The role of comparison. *Reading Horizons, 33,* 379–388.

Beach, R. (1993). *A teacher's introduction to reader-response theories.* Urbana, IL: National Council of Teachers of English.

Berk, L. E. (2003). *Child development* (6th ed.). Boston: Allyn & Bacon.

Bettelheim, B. (1976). *The uses of enchantment: The meaning and importance of fairy tales.* New York: Alfred A. Knopf.

Bishop, R. S. (Ed.). (1994). *Kaleidoscope: A multicultural booklist for grades K–8.* Urbana, IL: National Council of Teachers of English.

Brett, B. M., & Huck, C. S. (1982). Research update: Children's literature—the search for excellence. *Language Arts, 59,* 877–882.

Cai, M., & Traw, R. (1997). Literary literacy. *Journal of Children's Literature, 23*(2), 20–33.

Calkins, L. M. (2001). *The art of teaching reading.* New York: Longman.

Carr, J. (Ed.) (1982). *Beyond fact: Nonfiction for children and young people.* Chicago: American Library Association.

Chambers, A. (1983). *Introducing books to children.* Boston: Horn Book.

Chomsky, C. (1972). Stages in language development and reading exposure. *Harvard Educational Review, 42,* 1–39.

Cianciolo, P. (1995). Teaching and learning critical aesthetic responses to literature. In M. R. Sorensen & B. A. Lehman (Eds.), *Teaching with children's books: Paths to literature-based instruction* (pp. 144–158). Urbana, IL: National Council of Teachers of English.

Clay, M. (1979). *The early detection of reading difficulties.* Auckland, New Zealand: Heinemann.

Cohen, D. H. (1968). The effect of literature on vocabulary and reading achievement. *Elementary English, 45,* 209–213, 217.

Copenhaver, J. F. (2001). Listening to their voices connect literary and cultural understandings: Responses to small group read-alouds of *Malcolm X: A Fire Burning Brightly. The New Advocate, 14,* 343–359.

Coughlin, W. F., & Desilets, B. (1980). Frederick the field mouse meets advanced reading skills as children's literature goes to high school. *Journal of Reading, 24,* 207–211.

Cox, C., & Many, J. E. (1992). Toward an understanding of the aesthetic response to literature. *Language Arts, 69,* 28–33.

Crook, P. R. (1995). Decisions about curriculum in a literature-based program. In M. R. Sorensen & B. A. Lehman (Eds.), *Teaching with children's books: Paths to literature-based instruction* (pp. 70–80). Urbana, IL: National Council of Teachers of English.

Crook, P. R., & Lehman, B. A. (1991). Themes for two voices: Children's fiction and nonfiction as "whole literature." *Language Arts, 68,* 34–41.

Eeds, M., & Peterson, R. (1991). Teacher as curator: Learning to talk about literature. *The Reading Teacher, 45,* 118–126.

Eeds, M., & Peterson, R. (1994). Teachers as readers: Learning to talk about literature. *Journal of Children's Literature, 20,* 23–27.

Fenner, L. J. (1995). Assessment in a literature-based classroom. In M. R. Sorensen & B. A. Lehman (Eds.), *Teaching with children's books: Paths to literature-based instruction* (pp. 240–257). Urbana, IL: National Council of Teachers of English.

Fish, S. (1980). *Is there a text in this class? The authority of interpretive communities.* Cambridge, MA: Harvard University Press.

Fractor, J. S., Woodruff, M. C., Martinez, M. G., & Teale, W. H. (1993). Let's not miss opportunities to promote voluntary reading: Classroom libraries in the elementary school. *The Reading Teacher, 46,* 476–484.

Freeman, E. B., Lehman, B. A., & Scharer, P. L. (1995). *Suspenseful stories: A conversational exploration of literary qualities in nonfiction for children.* San Diego, CA: National Council of Teachers of English Convention.

Freeman, E. B., & Person, D. G. (1998). *Connecting informational children's books with content area learning.* Boston: Allyn & Bacon.

Fresch, M. J. (1995). Self-selected books of beginning readers: Standing before the smorgasbord. In M. R. Sorensen & B. A. Lehman (Eds.), *Teaching with children's books: Paths to literature-based instruction* (pp. 121–128). Urbana, IL: National Council of Teachers of English.

Frew, A. W. (1990). Four steps toward literature-based reading. *Journal of Reading, 34,* 98–102.

Frye, N. (1957). *Anatomy of criticism: Four essays.* Princeton, NJ: Princeton University Press.

Galda, L., & Cullinan, B. E. (2006). *Literature and the child* (6th ed.). Belmont, CA: Wadsworth/Thomson.

Gillet, J. W., Temple, C., & Crawford, A. N. (2004). *Understanding reading problems: Assessment and instruction* (6th ed.). Boston: Allyn & Bacon.

Goodman, K. (1986). *What's whole in whole language?* Portsmouth, NH: Heinemann.

Goodman, K. S., Shannon, P., Freeman, Y. S., & Murphy, S. (1988). *Report card on basal readers.* Katonah, NY: Richard C. Owen.

Goodman, Y. (1989). Evaluation of students: Evaluation of teachers. In K. S. Goodman, Y. M. Goodman, & W. J. Hood (Eds.), *The whole language evaluation book* (pp. 3–14). Portsmouth, NH: Heinemann.

Hade, D. D. (1991). Being literary in a literature-based classroom. *Children's Literature in Education, 22,* 1–17.

Hade, D. D. (1997). Reading multiculturally. In Violet J. Harris (Ed.), *Using multiethnic literature in the K–8 classroom* (pp. 233–256). Norwood, MA: Christopher-Gordon.

Hancock, M. R. (2004). *A celebration of literature and response: Children, books, and teachers in K–8 classrooms* (2nd ed.). Upper Saddle River, NJ: Pearson.

Harris, V. J. (1994). Multiculturalism and children's literature: An evaluation of ideology, publishing, curricula, and research. In C. K. Kinzer & D. J. Leu (Eds.), *Multidimensional aspects of literacy research, theory, and practice* (pp. 15–27). Chicago, IL: 43rd Yearbook of the National Reading Conference.

Hepler, S. (1988). Reading between the guide lines. *Children's Literature in Education, 19,* 55–62.

Hickman, J. (1981). A new perspective on response to literature: Research in an elementary school setting. *Research in the Teaching of English, 15,* 343–354.

Hill, B. C., Johnson, N. J., & Noe, K. L. S. (1995). *Literature circles and response.* Norwood, MA: Christopher-Gordon.

Hirsch, E. D., Jr., & Holdren, J. (Eds.).(1996). *Books to build on: A grade-by-grade resource guide for parents and teachers.* Buena Park, CA: Delta.

Holdaway, D. (1979). *Foundations of literacy.* Portsmouth, NH: Heinemann.

Huck, C. S., Kiefer, B. Z., Hepler, S., & Hickman, J. (2004). *Children's literature in the elementary school* (8th ed.). Boston: McGraw-Hill.

Iser, W. (1978). *The act of reading: A theory of aesthetic response.* Baltimore: Johns Hopkins University Press.

Jobe, R. (1993). *Cultural connections: Using literature to explore world cultures with children.* Markham, Ontario: Pembroke.

Kasten, W. C., Kristo, J. V., & McClure, A. A. (2005). *Living literature: Using children's literature to support reading and language arts.* Upper Saddle River, NJ: Pearson/Merrill Prentice Hall.

Kiefer, B. Z., Hepler, S., & Hickman, J. (2007). *Charlotte's Huck's children's literature* (9th ed.). Boston: McGraw-Hill.

Langer, J. A. (1995). *Envisioning literature: Literary understanding and literature instruction.* New York: Teachers College Press.

Latham, D. (2002). Childhood under siege: Lois Lowry's *Number the stars* and *The giver. The Lion and the Unicorn, 26,* 1–15.

Lehman, B. A. (1986). Children's choice and critical acclaim in literature for children. (Doctoral dissertation, University of Virginia, 1986). *Dissertation Abstracts International, 48* (05A), 1137.

Lehman, B. A. (2005). Religious representation in children's literature: Disclosure through character, perspective, and authority. In D. L. Henderson & J. P. May (Eds.), *Exploring culturally diverse literature for children and adolescents: Learning to listen in new ways* (pp. 11–21). Boston: Allyn & Bacon.

Lehman, B. A., & Crook, P. R. (1998). Doubletalk: A literary pairing of *The giver* and *We are all in the dumps with Jack and Guy. Children's Literature in Education, 29,* 69–78.

Lehman, B. A., Freeman, E. B., & Allen, V. G. (1994). Children's literature and literacy instruction: "Literature-based" elementary teachers' beliefs and practices. *Reading Horizons, 35,* 3–29.

Lehman, B. A., & Scharer, P. L. (1995–1996). Teachers' perspectives on response comparisons when children and adults read children's literature. *Reading Research and Instruction, 35,* 142–152.

Lepman, J. (2002). *A bridge of children's books.* Dublin, Ireland: O'Brien Press.

Lukens, R. J. (2003). *A critical handbook of children's literature* (7th ed.). Boston: Allyn & Bacon.

Many, J. E. (1990). The effect of reader stance on students' personal understanding of literature. In J. Zutell & S. McCormick (Eds.), *Literacy theory and research: Analyses from multiple paradigms, 39th Yearbook* (pp. 51–63). Chicago: National Reading Conference.

Many, J. E. (1991). The effects of stance and age level on children's literary responses. *Journal of Reading Behavior, 23,* 61–85.

Many, J. E., & Wiseman, D. L. (1992). The effect of teaching approach on third-grade students' response to literature. *Journal of Reading Behavior, 24,* 265–287.

May, J. P. (1995). *Children's literature and critical theory: Reading and writing for understanding.* New York: Oxford University Press.

McCormick, S. (1977). Should you read aloud *to* your children? *Language Arts,* *54*, 139–143, 163.

Moon, B. (1999). *Literary terms: A practical glossary.* Urbana, IL: National Council of Teachers of English.

Morrow, L. M. (1982). Relationships between literature programs, library corner designs, and children's use of literature. *Journal of Educational Research, 75,* 339–344.

Moss, B. (1991). Children's nonfiction trade books: A complement to content area texts. *The Reading Teacher, 45,* 26–32.

Moss, J. F. (1996). *Teaching literature in the elementary school: A thematic approach.* Norwood, MA: Christopher-Gordon.

Moss, J. F. (2002). *Literary discussion in the elementary school.* Urbana, IL: National Council of Teachers of English.

Neumeyer, P. F. (1994). *We are all in the dumps with Jack and Guy: Two nursery rhymes with pictures* by Maurice Sendak. *Children's Literature in Education, 25,* 29–40.

Nodelman, P. (1996). *The pleasures of children's literature* (2nd ed.). White Plains, NY: Longman.

Nodelman, P., & Reimer, M. (2003). *The pleasures of children's literature* (3rd ed.). Boston: Allyn & Bacon.

Norton, D. E. (1982). Using a webbing process to develop children's literature units. *Language Arts, 59,* 348–356.

Oxley, P. (1995). Literary tapestry: An integrated primary curriculum. In M. R. Sorensen & B. A. Lehman (Eds.), *Teaching with children's books: Paths to literature-based instruction* (pp. 213–217). Urbana, IL: National Council of Teachers of English.

Pappas, C. C., Kiefer, B. Z., & Levstik, L. S. (1999). An integrated language perspective in the elementary school: An action approach (3rd ed.). New York: Longman.

Pantaleo, S. (1995). The influence of teacher practice on student response to literature. *Journal of Children's Literature, 21*(1), 38–46.

Peters, D. (1995). Journey from hypocrisy: The teacher as reader becomes a teacher of readers. In M. R. Sorensen & B. A. Lehman (Eds.), *Teaching with children's books: Paths to literature-based instruction* (pp. 34–37). Urbana, IL: National Council of Teachers of English.

Peterson, R., & Eeds, M. (1990). *Grand conversations: Literature groups in action.* New York: Scholastic.

Pinsent, P. (2002). Fate and fortune in a modern fairy tale: Louis Sachar's *Holes.* *Children's Literature in Education, 33,* 203–212.

Popp, M. S. (1996). *Teaching language and literature in elementary classrooms: A resource book for professional development.* Mahwah, NJ: Lawrence Erlbaum.

Purves, A. C. (1990). Can literature be rescued from reading? In E. J. Farrell & J. R. Squire (Eds.), *Transactions with literature: A fifty-year perspective* (pp. 79–93). Urbana, IL: National Council of Teachers of English.

Reasoner, C. F. (1976). *Portfolio of working materials for individualized instruction.* Englewood Cliffs, NJ: Prentice-Hall.

Reutzel, D. R., & Cooter, R. B., Jr. (1991). Organizing for effective instruction: The reading workshop. *The Reading Teacher, 44,* 548–554.

Robb, L. (2000). *Teaching reading in middle school.* New York: Scholastic.

Roe, B. D., Smith, S. H., & Burns, P. C. (2005). *Teaching reading in today's elementary schools* (9th ed.). Boston: Houghton Mifflin.

Rosenblatt, L. M. (1938/1995). *Literature as exploration.* New York: Modern Language Association.

Rosenblatt, L. M. (1974). A way of happening. In R. B. Ruddell, E. J. Ahern, E. K. Hartson, & J. Taylor (Eds.), *Resources in reading-language instruction* (pp. 350–359). Englewood Cliffs, NJ: Prentice-Hall.

Rosenblatt, L. M. (1978). *The reader, the text, the poem: The transactional theory of the literary work.* Carbondale, IL: Southern Illinois University Press.

Rosenblatt, L. M. (1980). "What facts does this poem teach you?" *Language Arts, 57,* 386–394.

Rosenblatt, L. M. (1991). Literature—S.O.S.! *Language Arts, 68,* 444–448.

Roser, N. L. (2001). A place for everything and literature in its place. *The New Advocate, 14,* 211–221.

Scharer, P. L. (Guest ed.) (1992). Can you get there from here? One school's journey from basals to books (themed issue). *Literacy Matters, 4*(2).

Scharer, P. L. (1995). Making the move from basals to trade books: Taking the plunge. In M. R. Sorensen & B. A. Lehman (Eds.), *Teaching with children's books: Paths to literature-based instruction* (pp. 137–143). Urbana, IL: National Council of Teachers of English.

Scharer, P. L., Freeman, E. B., Lehman, B. A., & Allen, V. G. (1993). Literacy and literature in elementary classrooms: Teachers' beliefs and practices. In D. J. Leu & C. K. Kinzer (Eds.) *Examining central issues in literacy research, theory, and practice: 42nd Yearbook* (pp. 359–366). Chicago: National Reading Conference.

Scharer, P. L., Lehman, B. A., & Peters, D. (2001). Pondering the significance of big and little or saving the whales: Discussions of narrative and expository text in fourth- and fifth-grade classrooms. *Reading Research and Instruction, 40,* 297–314.

Short, K. G. (1999). The search for "balance" in a literature-rich curriculum. *Theory into Practice, 38,* 130–137.

Sipe, L. R. (1996). The private and public worlds of *We are all in the dumps with Jack and Guy. Children's Literature in Education, 27,* 87–108.

Sipe, L. R. (1997). Children's literature, literacy, and literary understanding. *Journal of Children's Literature, 23*(2), 6–19.

Sipe, L. R. (1998). Individual literary response styles of first and second graders. *National Reading Conference Yearbook, 47,* 76–89.

Sipe, L. R. (2000). "Those two gingerbread boys could be brothers": How children use intertextual connections during storybook readalouds. *Children's Literature in Education, 31,* 73–90.

Sipe, L. R. (2001). A palimpsest of stories: Young children's construction of intertextual links among fairytale variants. *Reading Research and Instruction, 40,* 333–352.

Sipe, L. R. (2002). Talking back and taking over: Young children's expressive engagement during storybook read-alouds. *The Reading Teacher, 55,* 476–483.

Sloan, G. D. (2003). *The child as critic: Teaching literature in elementary and middle schools* (4th ed.). New York: Teachers College Press.

Smith, F. (1996). *Reading without nonsense* (3rd ed.). New York: Teachers College Press.

Sorensen, M. R. (1995a). Developing a teaching guide for literary teaching. In M. R. Sorensen & B. A. Lehman (Eds.), *Teaching with children's books: Paths to literature-based instruction* (pp. 90–105). Urbana, IL: National Council of Teachers of English.

Sorensen, M. R. (1995b). Support groups for literature-based teaching. In M. R. Sorensen & B. A. Lehman (Eds.), *Teaching with children's books: Paths to literature-based instruction* (pp. 260–264). Urbana, IL: National Council of Teachers of English.

Stauffer, R. G. (1969). *Teaching reading as a thinking process.* New York: Harper & Row.

Sychterz, T. (2002). Rethinking childhood innocence. *The New Advocate, 15,* 183–195.

Temple, C., & Gillet, J. (1996). *Language and literacy: A lively approach.* New York: HarperCollins.

Tompkins, G. E. (1995). Hear ye, hear ye, and learn the lesson well: Fifth graders read and write about the American Revolution. In M. R. Sorensen & B. A. Lehman (Eds.), *Teaching with children's books: Paths to literature-based instruction* (pp. 171–187). Urbana, IL: National Council of Teachers of English.

Trites, R. S. (1997). *Waking Sleeping Beauty: Feminist voices in children's novels.* Iowa City: University of Iowa Press.

Tucker, N. (1972). How children respond to fiction. *Children's Literature in Education, 9,* 48–56.

Valencia, S. W., & Lipson, M. Y. (1998). Thematic instruction: A quest for challenging ideas and meaningful learning. In T. E. Raphael & K. H. Au (Eds.), *Literature-based instruction: Reshaping the curriculum* (pp. 95–122). Norwood, MA: Christopher-Gordon.

Vardell, S. M., & Jacobson, J. E. (1997). Teachers as readers: A status report. *Journal of Children's Literature, 23*(1), 16–25.

Watson, J. S. (2001). Appreciating Gantos' Jack Henry as an archetype. *The New Advocate, 14,* 379–385.

Wells, G. (1986). *The meaning makers: Children learning language and using language to learn.* Portsmouth, NH: Heinemann.

Willinsky, J. (1998). Teaching literature is teaching in theory. *Theory into Practice,*
    37, 244–250.
Wolf, S. A., Carey, A. A., & Mieras, E. L. (1996). "What is this literachurch stuff
    anyway?": Preservice teachers' growth in understanding children's literary
    response. *Reading Research Quarterly, 31,* 130–157.
Wollman-Bonilla, J. E., & Werchadlo, B. (1999). Teacher and peer roles in scaf-
    folding first graders' responses to literature. *The Reading Teacher, 52,* 598–
    607.
Woodward, A., Elliott, D. L., & Nagel, K. C. (1986). Beyond textbooks in elemen-
    tary social studies. *Social Education, 50,* 50–53.

Index

About the Author

BARBARA A. LEHMAN is professor of teaching and learning at Ohio State University, where she teaches graduate courses in children's literature and literacy at the Mansfield campus. She coedited *Teaching with Children's Books: Paths to Literature-Based Instruction* (1995) and coauthored *Global Perspectives in Children's Literature* (2001). She has had articles published in *ChLA Quarterly, Children's Literature in Education,* the *Journal of Children's Literature,* and other journals. She has coedited the *Journal of Children's Literature* and *Bookbird: A Journal of International Children's Literature.* She has served on and chaired book and author award committees, such as NCTE's Award for Excellence in Poetry for Children Committee, the Children's Literature Assembly's Notable Books in the Language Arts Committee, the Hans Christian Andersen Award U.S. nominating committee, the USBBY's Astrid Lindgren Memorial Award nominating committee, the International Reading Association's Arbuthnot Award Committee, and the Notable Books for a Global Society Committee. She was a Fulbright scholar in South Africa in 2004–2005. Her scholarly interests focus on multicultural and global children's literature and child-centered literary criticism.